100 facts
Magic & Mystery

Carey Scott

Consultant: Fiona Macdonald

Miles Kelly

First published in 2009 by Miles Kelly Publishing Ltd
Harding's Barn, Bardfield End Green, Thaxted, Essex, CM6 3PX

Copyright © Miles Kelly Publishing Ltd 2009

This edition printed 2012

4 6 8 10 9 7 5

Publishing Director: Belinda Gallagher
Creative Director: Jo Cowan
Assistant Editor: Carly Blake
Volume Designer: Sally Lace
Image Manager: Lorraine King
Indexer: Jane Parker
Production Manager: Elizabeth Collins
Reprographics: Ian Paulyn, Thom Allaway
Assets: Lorraine King

ISBN 978-1-84810-170-8

Printed in China

British Library Cataloguing-in-Publication Data
A catalogue record for this book is available from the British Library

ACKNOWLEDGEMENTS
The publishers would like to thank the following artists
who have contributed to this book:

Mike Foster, Andrea Morandi, Mike White
Cover artwork: Mike White
All other artwork from the Miles Kelly Artwork Bank

The publishers would like to thank the following
sources for the use of their photographs:

Page 6 © New Line Cinema/Everett/Rex Features; 8(b) National Geographic/Getty Images; 9 Action Press/Rex Features;
10(c) Science Photo Library; 11(t) © Hulton-Deutsch Collection/Corbis, (b) Getty Images; 12 New Line Cinema/The Kobal Collection;
13(t) © The Print Collector/Alamy, (b) © Dover Pictorial Archive; 17 © sharply_done/Fotolia.com; 20 Rex Features;
22(t) John Hooper/Hoopix®/MoW, (b) © Mikhail Lukyanov/Fotolia.com; 23 © Lindsay Hebberd/Corbis; 24–25 Getty Images;
24(b) © prints2buy/Fotolia.com; 25 © Jgz/Fotolia.com; 27 Bob Langrish; 28(b) © Alison Wright/Corbis, (t) © Uros Petrovic/Fotolia.com;
31(t) © Elena Butinova/Fotolia.com, (c) © Maksym Gorpenyuk/Fotolia.com, (b) John Hooper/Hoopix®/MoW;
32 © Sebastian Kaulitzki/Fotolia.com, (t) John Hooper/Hoopix®/MoW; 33(b) © New Line Cinema/Everett/Rex Features;
35(t) The Granger Collection/Topfoto/TopFoto.co.uk; 37(t) © Mary Evans Picture Library/Alamy,
(b) © Warner Brothers/Photos 12/Alamy; 38 (background) © laxmi/Fotolia.com, (b) © Warner Brothers/Photos 12/Alamy;
39(b) © Universal Pictures/Photos 12/Alamy; 40 © Walt Disney Pictures/Topfoto/TopFoto.co.uk; 41(t) © PoodlesRock/Corbis;
42(b) NMeM/Science & Society; 43(c) © Bettmann/Corbis, (b) Quilici/Iverson/Rex Features; 44–45 © scol22/Fotolia.com;
45 © Robbie Jack/Corbis, (t) © dmitry_kim/Fotolia.com; 46(t) Dimitris Legakis/Rex Features, (c) © Anyka/Fotolia.com,
(b) ©1999 Credit:Topham Picturepoint/TopFoto.co.uk; 47 Erik Pendzich/Rex Features

All other photographs are from:

Corel, digitalSTOCK, digitalvision, Fotolia.com, iStockphoto.com, John Foxx,
PhotoAlto, PhotoDisc, PhotoEssentials, PhotoPro, Stockbyte

Made with paper from a sustainable forest

www.mileskelly.net
info@mileskelly.net

www.factsforprojects.com

Contents

What is magic? 6

History of magic 8

Magical practices 10

People with magical powers 12

Alchemy 14

Making predictions 16

Spells and ceremonies 18

Helpful magic 20

Harmful magic 22

Magical places 24

Animal magic 26

Healers and healing 28

Prized plants 30

Tools, amulets and charms 32

Symbols 34

Famous magic-makers 36

Mischievous magic 38

Magical lands 40

Magical events 42

Superstition 44

Illusionist magic 46

Index 48

What is magic?

1 **Throughout history and all over the world, people have believed in magic.** The word 'magic' describes powers or events that are beyond scientific understanding. Belief in magic probably began as a way of explaining seemingly mysterious events, such as earthquakes, disease or a run of good luck. Magic has always formed a part of religious beliefs, for example, as supernatural beings called gods. Different magical ideas are also found in the popular beliefs and traditions of a culture, called folklore.

▲ J R R Tolkien's fantasy novel *The Lord of the Rings* (1954) is one of the most popular magical stories ever written. This scene from the 2002 film *The Lord of the Rings: The Two Towers* shows the good wizard Gandalf the White returning to meet his friends.

History of magic

2 **It is likely that belief in magic originated in prehistoric times.** Cave paintings in Europe and North Africa depict scenes that may show magical rituals. By around 5000 years ago, when people began recording their beliefs in writing, magic was part of their lives.

▲ This drawing of a 10,000-year-old cave painting in France may show a figure performing a magical dance.

3 **In ancient civilizations such as Greece and Rome, magic was a part of everyday life.** Most people believed that invisible beings existed, that the future could be predicted and that magical events occurred.

▼ In the 1600s, Isaac Newton began to dispel magical beliefs by showing that rainbows were made by sunlight being scattered into many colours by water drops, or glass.

4 **During the medieval period (500–1450), and up to about 1700, most Europeans believed in witchcraft.** Some scientists and scholars practised magic along with sciences such as mathematics. Yet by around 1800, developments in chemistry and physics were able to explain many events and natural phenomena once thought to be magical, such as rainbows.

QUIZ

1. Who were the first people to believe in magic?
2. What did Isaac Newton discover in the 1600s?
3. What do shamans do?

Answers:
1. Prehistoric people
2. Rainbows are caused by sunlight being split into different colours 3. Carry out magical healing

5 In the modern world, magic has lost much of its power, but it has not disappeared. Fortune-telling, especially astrology, is still popular. Magical healing lives on in some alternative medicines. Yet for most people, the word 'magic' means tricks of illusion performed by stage magicians rather than supernatural powers.

▲ A popular stage magic trick is to create the illusion of levitation – a person rising into the air without any visible support.

6 In traditional beliefs in some parts of the world, magic still survives today. Among native North Americans and in parts of Asia and Africa, shamans, (spiritual healers) carry out traditional healing in their local communities. Magicians and witches can be found even in urban places, such as the cities of Brazil and South Africa.

Magical practices

7 The three main types of magical practice are divination, magic spells and high magic. Divination is the use of magic to predict the future or discover knowledge. Magic spells are used to achieve specific results. High magic aims to gain control over nature through magical knowledge.

8 Astrology is a well known form of divination. Astrologists believe that the positions of the Sun, Moon, stars and planets influence peoples' lives, and can be used to predict the future. Astrology began in the ancient world and spread to many different countries.

Love spell

On Midsummer's Eve, pick a red rose and wrap it in white silk. Hide it away in a safe place until Christmas. Then open the silk and if the flower is still intact, wear it on your person. The first person to admire it will fall in love with you.

▲ People have used spells to make others fall in love with them for thousands of years, such as this simple white (good) magic love spell.

9 Magic spells aim to help someone achieve a particular result. A spell may be intended to heal or harm a person, or make them fall in love. It may also give protection against harmful magic. Often magic spells are passed on by word of mouth, but they have also been written down.

10 Those who practise high magic aim to understand and control the world. Magicians of 15th- and 16th-century Europe spent years reading ancient books on magic, attending meetings on the subject and taking part in magic rituals. They believed that magic was the key to understanding the secrets of nature, and that mastering it would make them as powerful as gods.

▲ Italian philosopher Giovanni Pico della Mirandola (1463–1494) became interested in high magic after studying ancient magical texts.

◄ This 17th-century illustration shows an astrologer casting someone's horoscope. A personal horoscope might list auspicious (lucky) days.

11 Magic-makers have different names. Shamans use magic to cure illness, but they make spells and practise high magic too. Diviners practise various kinds of divination. Witches cast magic spells, and magicians are interested in high magic.

◄ Diviners called 'dowsers' search for water using metal or wooden rods, or pendulums. In Tehuacán, Mexico, a farmer claims he has developed a water-divining method using just a rock dangling from a thin rope.

QUIZ

1. What are the three magical practices?
2. How do astrologists predict the future?
3. Who practises high magic?

Answers:
1. Divination, magic spells, high magic 2. By studying the positions of the Sun, Moon, stars and planets 3. Magicians and shamans

People with magical powers

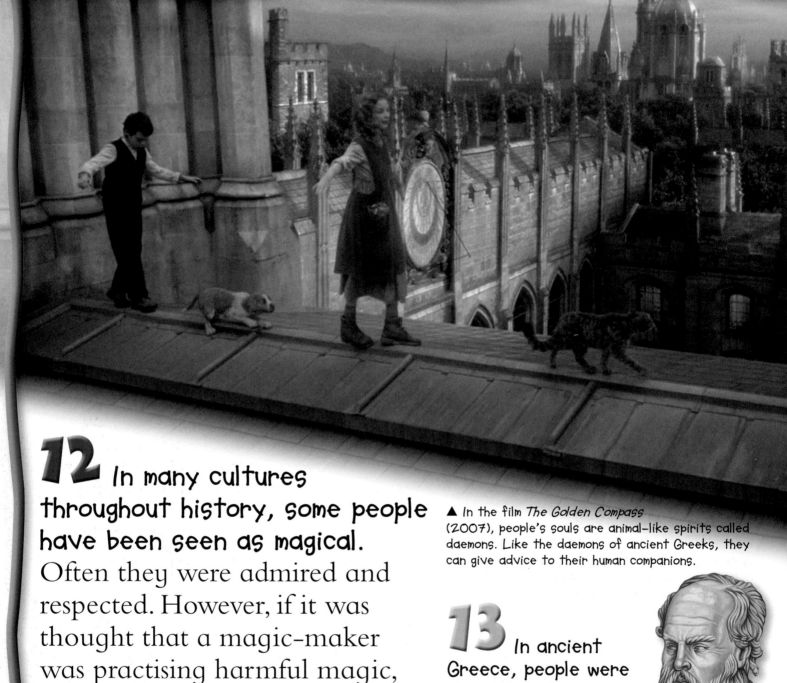

12 In many cultures throughout history, some people have been seen as magical. Often they were admired and respected. However, if it was thought that a magic-maker was practising harmful magic, they might be severely punished.

▲ In the film *The Golden Compass* (2007), people's souls are animal-like spirits called daemons. Like the daemons of ancient Greeks, they can give advice to their human companions.

Socrates (469–399 BC)

13 In ancient Greece, people were thought to have access to magical beings. They believed that everyone had a protecting magical spirit, called a daemon, which accompanied them through life. The most well known daemon belonged to Socrates and it was thought to advise its master against doing anything dangerous.

I DON'T BELIEVE IT!

In Europe, between 1400–1650, elderly women living alone, especially those with pets, were likely to be accused of being witches.

14 **In ancient and modern times, rulers have been seen as magical.** In ancient Egypt, people thought the pharaoh had so much power he could make the earth tremble by raising his hand. Until 1945, emperors of Japan were seen as living gods descended from the Sun goddess Amaterasu. In some religious beliefs, rulers are closer to gods than ordinary people.

▶ Emperor Hirohito, shown here in his coronation robes, rejected his divine status after Japan's defeat in World War II (1939–1945).

15 **In Europe, for more than 200 years, people were executed if they were thought to be witches.** Many thousands of people were hanged, drowned or burned for practising harmful magic. Some experts think witchcraft was invented to persecute people who did not fit into society.

▼ In 1612, during the Lancashire witch trials in England, ten people were found guilty of murder by witchcraft and hanged.

▲ One reason shamans wear costumes is to emphasize their powers when conducting rituals and ceremonies.

16 **Only people thought to have magical powers can be shamans.** As well as being able to see into the future, shamans communicate with spirits, which enables them to be healers. Shamans gain their powers through a natural 'calling', or through experiences, such as illness.

Alchemy

17 Alchemy was a scientific and magical art, which aimed to change common metals into gold. It was first practised in the ancient world. Ancient Greek philosopher Aristotle taught that all matter was made up of four elements, and altering their amounts could change one substance into another.

Cauldron

19 Alchemists did not want to make gold to become rich. They saw gold as the most perfect, pure substance. Having the ability to turn ordinary metals, such as lead, into pure gold was thought to have a similar effect on the alchemist – he would be turned into a higher being.

18 The alchemist's main aim was to find the Philosopher's Stone. Alchemists thought that only this magical substance could change metal into gold. An elixir made from the stone was also thought to grant eternal life. But the alchemists searched in vain.

Glass still

Bellows

Animal skull

▼ An alchemist's laboratory was often hidden away in the cellar or attic of his home, and would have been cluttered with equipment to carry out experiments.

20 When magic failed, alchemists used trickery. Their most common trick was to conceal gold in the stick they used to stir the molten metal, so it looked as though gold was being produced.

Alchemical textbook

Pestle and mortar

Dishes of dried plants and powdered substances

21 Alchemists made major scientific breakthroughs. They found ways of refining metals, and first described important substances such as hydrochloric acid and arsenic. They made their discoveries by carrying out experiments in laboratories, just as chemists do today.

Making predictions

22 There are over 50 ways of predicting, or divining, the future. Some divination methods look for signs of warning or guidance to help with making decisions and answering questions. Other methods include fortune-telling, which tries to discover an individual's future.

▼ The most important oracle in ancient Greece was at Delphi. The priestess at the temple of Apollo would go into a trance. The god then spoke through her, giving magical words of advice.

23 The ancient Greeks used divination to help them make important decisions. If a general was thinking about going to war or considering marriage, he consulted an oracle. This was a place where a priestess in a temple was thought to be able to see the future by communicating with the temple god.

▶ Ancient Chinese diviners recorded their predictions on bones in an early form of Chinese writing.

▶ Telling the future by studying the flight patterns and cries of birds is called augury.

24 More than 3000 years ago, the Shang kings of ancient China relied on a method of divination that used animal bones. The king went to see a diviner with a particular question. The diviner inscribed the question on the bone and then heated it until the bone cracked. The answer to the king's question was 'read' from the cracks formed by the heat.

25 Tasseographers see a person's future in the patterns in tea leaves or coffee grounds. Tea-leaf reading started in the ancient world. A tasseographer looks for certain shapes in the tea leaves, which mean particular things. Seeing the shape of a house means change and success, but a mountain foresees obstruction.

▶ In palmistry, the most prominent four lines on the hand are called the heart line, head line, life line and fate line. The right hand is read unless the person is left-handed.

PALM LINES
1. Life line Length and vitality of a person's life
2. Head line Mentality and intelligence
3. Heart line Emotions
4. Fate line Fortune and success

26 Palm reading is the art of reading a person's character and future from the lines on their hands. It was first practised over 5000 years ago in India. In the 1900s, a palm-reading craze swept the USA and Britain, and palm-readers read the hands of the British royal family and Hollywood stars.

Spells and ceremonies

▼ In William Shakespeare's play *Macbeth*, three witches tend to a cauldron of poisonous–looking potion. As they add ingredients, they chant the spell 'Double, double, toil and trouble, fire burn, and cauldron bubble'.

27 **What is a magic spell?** It is a set of words to be spoken or chanted, often during a ritual of some kind. If the magic spell is directed at a particular person, then using their name, or having a personal possession or a picture of them is thought to increase the power of it.

QUIZ

1. How can the power of a spell aimed at a particular person be increased?
2. In Cornwall, what were white witches known as?
3. In Mexico, what is celebrated every November?

Answers:
1. Saying the person's name, or using a personal possession or photograph 2. Pellars 3. The Day of the Dead

28
In medieval England, written spells were thought to be especially effective magic, probably because few people could write. In Cornwall, white witches called 'pellars' sold written spells as protection against harmful magic. For best results, pellars recommended placing their spells under a pillow.

29
In mainland Europe, from the 18th to 20th centuries, people performed a ceremony to keep witches away. On May Eve (30th April) people ran around their houses and villages seven times, shouting 'Witch flee, flee from here, or it will go ill with thee'. In Germany, May Eve was a day for burning witches at the stake.

30
In Mexico, the Day of the Dead is celebrated in November. Ceremonies are held to encourage the souls of dead people to visit the living. People make offerings to the dead, including sugar skulls and sweets. The souls of the dead are said to consume the sweets' spiritual essence.

▶ This typical Day of the Dead altar is crowded with intricately decorated sugar skulls. The skeletons represent dead loved ones.

Helpful magic

► A Native American Indian performs a rain dance at a reservoir in Derbyshire, England, during a drought in 1995. Science has been unable to make rain, so people still occasionally put their faith in magic instead.

31 Ceremonies, spells and magic potions have all been used to try and ensure good fortune. Most helpful magic tries to encourage events that may happen anyway. But sometimes people have used magic to try to achieve things that exist only in their dreams, such as immortality.

32 From ancient Egypt to 21st-century North America, people have performed magic ceremonies in the hope of bringing rain. In May 2008, after a long drought in the state of Georgia, USA, Native Americans from the Shoshone, Cherokee and Muscogee nations gathered at a sacred site and performed a ceremony to bring rain.

33 Magic has been used to make a person fall in love. An example from a 10th-century Arabic book on magic called 'Picatrix', suggested putting two dolls in a fireplace and a piece of ice in the fire. When the ice melted, the lovers' hearts would supposedly melt too. This is imitative magic – it hopes to influence events by imitating them.

▲ The ancient legend of Tristan and Isolde tells how the pair fall in love after they accidentally drink a powerful love potion.

▲ Witchetty grubs are a useful source of protein for some indigenous Australian peoples.

34 In some cultures, magic is used to ensure a good supply of food. Indigenous peoples of central Australia eat an insect lava called a witchetty grub. They perform a ceremony that mimics the grub emerging from its chrysalis, to ensure there will be plenty of them to eat. In Mauritius, fishermen attach pictures of fish to trees on the beach to help them make a big catch.

I DON'T BELIEVE IT!

Until the 17th century, builders in England left water and bread inside the walls of cottages to ward off hunger for the people who would be living there.

35 Some magicians believed eternal life was possible. In medieval Europe, magicians thought that a potion called the Elixir of Life could grant the drinker eternal life. In ancient China, magician Wei Po-Yang claimed he had created a Pill of Immortality. The secret of eternal life is still looked for today – in science.

▼ Ouroboros – a dragon forming a circle by swallowing its own tail – is an ancient symbol of immortality.

Harmful magic

36 The idea of using a doll to magically harm a person has been known in cultures around the world. A magical link is thought to exist between the doll and the person it represents, so harming the doll harms the person too. Dolls were stuck with pins, but might also have been burned or boiled.

▲ This clay poppet doll from Cornwall, England, has had rows of small nails driven into its chest. This would have been intended to harm the person it represented.

▼ In medieval European folklore, a person's shadow represented their soul. People who had sold their souls to the devil were thought to cast no shadow.

37 It was thought that harming a person's shadow could harm the person too. In the 19th century, magicians of the island of Wetar, Indonesia, were said to be able to cause illness by stabbing a person's shadow. Into the 20th century, in parts of Central Africa and India, folklore said that spearing a person's shadow could kill them.

38 In medieval Europe, textbooks of magic began to appear. The books were called 'grimoires' and were written by magicians. They contained instructions for calling up and commanding supernatural beings that would carry out the magician's orders. Complicated ceremonies to summon up the beings were described in detail.

QUIZ

1. What were medieval magic textbooks called?
2. Who is born with magical powers — sorcerers or witches?
3. What is *ojo* commonly known as?

Answers:
1. Grimoires 2. Witches
3. The 'evil eye'

39 In some traditional African communities, sorcerers and witches use different forms of harmful magic. Sorcerers carry out magic with potions and magical objects and they learn magic from other sorcerers. Witches are born with magical powers and they can cause harm to someone just by concentrating bad feeling on them.

▶ In ancient Rome, people asked the gods to harm their enemies. They would leave a tablet inscribed with their foe's name and curse words at a temple.

40 Mexican folklore says that *ojo*, or 'evil eye', is a major cause of childhood illness. Today, some Mexicans still believe that common illnesses can be caused by an intense stare. A witch can deliberately cause *ojo*, but a person with very strong vision could also create *ojo* by accident.

▼ The Bhil people of India think that evil spirits cause illness. The black powder around this baby's eyes is to protect her against the 'evil eye'.

Magical places

41 Glastonbury Tor in England is believed to be a centre of mystical energy. The natural, cone-shaped hill has flattened steps, called terraces, shaped into it, which may be the remains of a maze used for religious rituals. The site is also said to be criss-crossed by tracks of magical energy called ley lines.

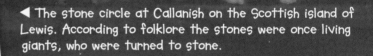

◀ The stone circle at Callanish on the Scottish island of Lewis. According to folklore the stones were once living giants, who were turned to stone.

42 In many parts of the world, early peoples built stone circles from boulders. Some historians think they were sacred burial grounds, or temples where magic may have been carried out. Another theory suggests that they helped people observe and map the movements of the Sun, Moon and stars.

43 For native Australian peoples, a sandstone mass is the most magical place on Earth. Uluru rises out of the central Australian desert and is thought to be crossed by magical 'dreaming tracks'. According to traditional belief, spirit ancestors created the tracks as they travelled the land, singing the world into existence.

▼ Glastonbury Tor is a 150-metre-high natural hill. At its top is St Michael's Tower, the remains of a medieval church.

44 In Celtic folklore, green mounds are entrances to the underworld. Magical beings lived in the underworld and Celtic people thought these beings could emerge from grassy mounds and interact with humans. It was thought that humans might be able to enter the underworld there too.

▶ A spider so big it can be seen fully only from the air is one of the animal drawings of the Nazca lines.

◀ The lone mountain of Uluru, also called Ayers Rock, is almost 350 metres high and measures 9.4 kilometres in circumference.

45 High on a desert-like plain in Peru, South America, lies one of the great mysteries of the world. Covering an incredible 500 square kilometres are hundreds of huge drawings of animals and plants, carved into the ground. The Nazca Lines, as they are known, were made around 2000 years ago. Some historians think they were made for gods in the sky to see. Others think the drawings were a kind of cosmic calendar.

Animal magic

46 In folklore, real and mythical animals can have magical powers. Animals may be good – folk tales from around the world tell of birds that give warnings or advice to humans. But they can also be evil, such as the dragon that terrorizes a town in the legend of Saint George and the Dragon.

47 Dragons are believed to control the forces of nature. In ancient Chinese folklore, these mythical animals are responsible for the running of the world. The Terrestrial Dragon looks after streams and rivers and can cause floods and droughts. The Divine Dragon controls winds and rain, and makes lightning by flashing its eyes.

▲ Legend says George killed the dragon that terrorized the people of Lydia (in modern Turkey).

▲ In Chinese mythology, dragons are helpful. Each Chinese New Year, dragon dances are performed to scare off evil spirits.

▶ Black cats are most commonly depicted as witches' familiars.

48 Animals could be witches' helpers. In medieval Europe, some people believed that spirits could live in animals' bodies. Called 'familiars', these animals could be witches' servants and companions. Frogs, snakes and spiders have been depicted as witches' familiars, as well as cats.

49 Animals were thought to be able to foresee death. Gaelic folklore tells that in 597 BC, Saint Columba sat down to rest, and a horse came up to him. Sensing that he was dying, it laid its head on his chest and cried. Saint Columba died soon after. A 16th-century English belief says that a dog scratching the floor and howling means that someone nearby is about to die. .

▶ The unicorn was imagined as a beautiful, dignified animal with a gentle nature.

50 The unicorn was a mythical horse–like animal with a horn on its forehead. Up until the 1700s, most Europeans believed the unicorn was real, but so shy and fast that it was impossible to catch. According to an ancient Greek text dating from the second century AD, a unicorn would calmly lie down and put its head in the lap of a beautiful young girl.

Healers and healing

51 Shamans of central and north Asia are thought to be able to cure illness by going into a trance and 'leaving' their bodies. They believe that disease is caused by a person's soul having been lost or stolen. The shaman's main task in healing is to find and capture the missing soul and return it to the patient's body.

▼ In Nepal, Asia, the Dami Jankris are shamans who carry out traditional healing. Dancing, chanting and drumming are used during healing ceremonies.

▶ All over the world, healers would be expected to know how to treat illnesses using simple herbs and other plants.

Dandelion leaves and root
Useful for treating liver complaints

52 In England, between the 16th and 20th centuries, villagers called Cunning Folk performed healing using herbs and spells. Cunning Folk knew enough about medicinal herbs to be effective healers. As well as curing illness, it was believed that their healing offered protection against witchcraft.

Never attempt to eat any of the plants mentioned in this book. They could seriously harm you.

Poppy seeds
Used to treat skin complaints, insomnia and to reduce inflammation

Mint leaves
Used to treat sickness and aid digestion

QUIZ

1. What does a shaman aim to do during healing?
2. What were England's village healers known as?
3. Which ancient Greek god was responsible for healing?

Answers:
1. Find the patient's soul and return it to their body 2. The Cunning Folk 3. Asklepios

53 In ancient Greece, it was believed that remedies for illnesses were revealed in dreams. Believers spent a night at the temple of Asklepios, the god of healing. As they slept, the god entered their dreams with suggestions of remedies. After each successful cure, the details of the illness and the treatment were written down, or carved on the temple walls to record them.

▶ The long tusks of the narwhal were commonly passed off as unicorn horns.

54 Some magical healing was thought to carry an illness away. Ancient Greek philosopher Democritus said that a person stung by a scorpion should sit on a donkey and whisper to it 'a scorpion has stung me' to transfer the pain to the animal. In medieval England, a patient was rubbed with an eggshell stuffed with horsehair. This was then thrown into the street to transfer the illness to whoever stepped on it.

55 It was believed that a unicorn's horn could neutralize snakebites, cure the plague and heal injuries. Horns that were thought to have been taken from unicorns were incredibly valuable. In 1553, a horn owned by the King of France was valued at £20,000 – £5 million today. But the King was deceived, for the horn probably came from a rhinoceros, or was the tusk of a narwhal, a type of whale.

Prized plants

Liverwort
Like the human liver, the leaves of liverwort have three lobes, so it was used for treating liver complaints

Walnuts
They look like brains — a sign they may be able to cure headaches

Bloodroot
The root contains red sap, so was used to treat blood ailments (even though it is dangerously poisonous)

56 **Plants held clues to their medicinal uses.** In the 1600s, the book *The Doctrine of Signatures* popularized the idea that God created every plant with a medicinal use. If people could read the signs of those uses, they would see which plants could treat which illnesses.

◀ According to author Jakob Böhme, a plant that resembles a part of the body could be used to treat disorders of that part. Names of many plants reflect this idea.

Lungwort
With spotty leaves that were thought to resemble infected lungs, this plant was used in the treatment of lung disorders

57 **Celtic priests called druids cut mistletoe in a special way to retain its magic.** A druid dressed in white robes cut the plant on the sixth day of the Moon's cycle using a gold sickle. He let it fall onto a white robe and placed the plant in water. The water could then be sprinkled around an area to protect it from evil.

Maidenhair fern
This plant looks as though it could encourage a healthy head of hair

◀ In Scottish folklore, touching someone suspected of being a witch with a rowan branch would ensure that the devil took them away.

I DON'T BELIEVE IT!

One traditional English love potion was a mixture of powdered periwinkle flowers and earthworms.

58 **The rowan tree, or mountain ash, was thought to protect against harmful magic.** In Celtic Europe, planting rowan trees around a house, or nailing a rowan branch over the door was thought to stop evil spirits from entering. Around 600 years ago, Viking sailors carried rowan-wood amulets for protection against the hostile Norse goddess of the sea, Ran.

◀ Today, mistletoe is used as a Christmas decoration as its pretty (but poisonous) white berries appear in winter.

59 **All over the world, people have eaten mushrooms in magic rituals.** Chemicals in some mushrooms are 'hallucinogenic'. This means that they affect a person's sense of reality, often causing colourful visions. Some magicians think that these effects help people to enter magical worlds.

60 **According to legend, the root of the mandrake plant uttered a deadly shriek when it was pulled from the ground.** To avoid being killed by the shriek, people made their dogs dig up the roots. Mandrake root was used in medieval magic rituals, as well as in medicine in central and southern Europe, where it grows natively.

◀ The mandrake root can look like an animal's body, and this one has been carved with the face of a monkey to emphasize the resemblance.

Tools, amulets and charms

61 The wand was a tool for aiming magic at a particular object. To ensure that a wand had magical qualities, it was supposed to be made of hazel wood cut from the tree at sunrise. A wand for harmful magic was supposed to be cut from a cypress tree at midnight.

▼ Wands were used by witches and magicians in all sorts of magical activities, such as transforming an animal or person into something else.

62 Amulets were thought to provide magical protection. They were usually small, carved objects of gods that were carried, or worn in jewellery. Some amulets protected against the 'evil eye', others helped women in childbirth and some protected specific parts of the body against injury.

▲ The ancient Romans gave a gold good luck charm called a bulla to their babies.

▶ The ancient Egyptian Eye of Horus was worn for protection and safety.

MAKE A MAGIC AMULET

You will need:
stiff card   scissors   felt-tip pen

1. Along the long edge of the card write the word ABRACADABRA, leaving space between each letter.
2. Underneath, starting just inside the first A, write ABRACADABR.
3. Carry on, each time missing off another letter at the end, until your last word is the letter A.
4. You should now have a cone shape of magic letters. Cut it out and put it up it in a special place.

In medieval times, the Abracadabra amulet was thought to protect against disease.

```
A B R A C A D A B R A
A B R A C A D A B R
A B R A C A D A B
A B R A C A D A
A B R A C A D
A B R A C A
A B R A C
A B R A
A B R
A B
A
```

◀ This amulet was carried by Viking warriors for strength.

64 In 16th-century England, many people thought rings could have magical properties. Inscriptions were believed to increase their magical properties – people wore rings inscribed with names of holy people to keep the plague and other illnesses away. The influential and successful Cardinal Wolsey was accused of bewitching King Henry VIII by giving him a magical ring.

◀ Even today, people nail horseshoes to their front doors to bring them good luck.

63 A horseshoe nailed to a door was believed to keep out evil spirits and witches. Iron horseshoes are lucky charms in all countries where horses are used. This is probably because blacksmiths are associated with magic. According to ancient folklore, they were taught metal-working by magical beings.

▶ Frodo reaches for The One Ring in the film *The Lord of the Rings: The Fellowship of the Ring* (2001). The magical ring makes the wearer invisible and forces him to enter a spirit world.

Famous magic-makers

71 **The most famous magician is Merlin.** Legendary advisor to British King Arthur, Merlin's powers included the ability to see the future. Legend says that Merlin used magic to arrange Arthur's birth and then to make sure he became king, because he knew Arthur would be a great ruler.

▼ Merlin as we recognize him today made his first appearance in stories by Geoffrey of Monmouth, written in the 12th century.

72 **Russian and East European folklore tells of a witch called Baba Yaga.** The old woman lives in a hut perched on giant chicken's feet. She flies through the air with a giant pestle and mortar, and kidnaps and cooks children in her enormous oven.

73 **Simon Magus, or Simon the Sorcerer, lived in the first century AD.** People believed he could fly, become invisible, appear as an animal – and even that he was a demon in disguise. This was probably because he went against accepted beliefs to start his own religion.

◄ Scholar John Dee (1527–1608) wrote several books about magic that he claimed were told to him by angels.

74 Scientist and mathematician John Dee was the most important magician of 16th-century England. As a young man he became an advisor to Queen Elizabeth I – he read her horoscope and used astrology to decide the day of her coronation. Later, he became interested in magic to gain knowledge about the secrets of life and nature.

75 In 13th-century Germany, scholar and magician Albertus Magnus was reported to have built a magical metal head that could answer any question. Magnus studied subjects including alchemy and astrology, and was so clever that people thought he must be capable of magical feats. However, the magical head was never found.

▶ In the film *Harry Potter and Order of the Phoenix* (2007), Harry uses his magical powers to battle the evil Lord Voldemort.

76 In modern times, magic-making lives on in J K Rowling's boy-wizard, Harry Potter. Among his magical powers are the ability to fly on a broomstick, conjure up objects, transport himself from one place to another and read people's minds. Harry uses his powers to battle against evil.

Mischievous magic

77 **In Celtic Europe, people began to believe that magical creatures lived in the woods around them.** These creatures became known as fairies. They were said to look like humans, but they posessed magical powers such as the ability to fly. Mostly, fairies' mischief was playful, but they could be unkind too.

▼ Since Victorian times (1837–1901), fairies have mostly been depicted as tiny girls with insect wings. In earlier times, they could be as tall as humans.

78 **In Scandinavian folklore, the hills and mountains were inhabited by elves.** Like fairies, elves could be unkind if offended. People thought they caused an irritating skin rash called elven blow, so they left offerings out for the elves to discourage any bad behaviour.

◄ The *Harry Potter* stories feature a good elf called Dobby, who becomes Harry's friend.

79 **In northern European folklore, hairy cannibals called trolls could sniff out humans with their large noses.** In some places, trolls were believed to be giants and in others dwarves, but all trolls were evil. However, they had one fatal weakness – if a person found out a troll's name, he or she could kill the troll just by saying it.

80 In Scottish folklore, mythical creatures called brownies helped around the house. It was thought that these little people appeared at night to carry out helpful deeds, and disappeared before dawn. In return people left out food and drink for them. In some villages there were special flat, thin stones called brownie's stones, where offerings were left.

81 Was there ever a race of tiny people? In 1892, folklore expert David MacRitchie suggested that fairylore might be based on real events. Perhaps there was once a race of small people who were forced into hiding as Celtic civilizations grew rich and powerful in Scotland, around 200 BC.

▶ The story of *The Borrowers* (1952) by Mary Norton is the first in a series of novels about a race of tiny people who live beneath the floor of a house and 'borrow' the things they need from humans.

Magical lands

▲ The wicked White Witch made sure it is always winter in the land of Narnia, as shown in the 2005 film *The Chronicles of Narnia: The Lion, the Witch and the Wardrobe.*

82 Children can only reach the land of Narnia through a magical wardrobe. Narnia is a fictional world inhabited by dwarves, mythical creatures and talking animals, and its ruler is a god-like lion called Aslan. This magical land was dreamt up by C S Lewis, and first featured in his children's book *The Lion, the Witch and the Wardrobe* in 1949.

IMAGINE A LAND

1. Find a quiet place and make sure you have a pen and paper.
2. Think of a name for your imaginary land and write it down.
3. Describe what your imaginary land looks like.
4. What creatures live there? They could be fairies or unicorns, or you could invent some creatures of your own. Give them names, too.
5. Think of a password to enter your imaginary land and write it down.

Keep your imaginary land secret — only share it with your best friends.

▶ Peter Pan, along with the fairy Tinkerbell and The Lost Boys, are the most well known inhabitants of Neverland — a paradise island where people do not grow old.

83 Scottish author J M Barrie invented a magical children's paradise called Neverland, in his play *Peter Pan*. The children who visit Neverland cannot grow older while they are there, and once grown-up they cannot return to Neverland. J M Barrie wanted Neverland to represent the imagination of children, and to show how it is lost with adulthood.

84 The ancient Egyptians believed in the existence of a dangerous magical underworld called Duat. They thought that dead people had to pass through Duat to reach the afterlife, where they would live forever. There were many dangers, such as poisonous snakes and lakes of fire. To help the dead get past these dangers, each of them was given a map, a set of magic spells and protective amulets.

Anubis

85 From the 12th to 17th centuries, some Europeans believed in a magical land ruled by a Christian king, somewhere in Asia or Africa. It was believed to be full of wonders, such as the Fountain of Youth — a natural spring with the power of making the old, young again. There were many expeditions to search for this land.

◀ Egyptian god Anubis was thought to help the souls of the dead enter Duat.

41

Superstition

90 **Much of the magic from the past lives on today in the form of superstitions and customs.** All cultures have their own superstitions, based on different beliefs. Some people believe in superstitions, others practise them out of habit, and some defy them on purpose to show they are not superstitious.

91 **Breaking a mirror brings seven years' bad luck.** This superstition comes from an ancient Roman idea that life renews itself every seven years. It was also believed that the reflected image represents the soul, and damaging it hurts the individual too. As mirrors were more commonly used in the 1500s, it became unlucky to break one.

▼ Here are some superstitions that are still alive today.

Good Luck

❀ **FOUR-LEAF CLOVERS**
Finding a four-leaf clover brings good luck.

❀ **KNOCKING ON WOOD**
To knock on wood when speaking of bad luck stops it from coming true.

❀ **PENNIES**
Finding a penny and picking it up will bring good luck for the rest of the day.

❀ **RABBIT'S FOOT**
Carrying a rabbit's foot brings good luck and protects the person from evil spirits.

❀ **CROSSING YOUR FINGERS**
Crossing your fingers wards off evil spirits and bad luck, and helps wishes come true.

Bad Luck

BLACK CATS
If a black cat crosses your path and walks away, it takes your good luck with it.

UMBRELLAS
Opening an umbrella indoors brings bad luck.

WALKING UNDER LADDERS
It is bad luck to walk under a leaning ladder.

MAGPIES
Seeing a lone magpie is a sign of bad luck because they stay with one mate for life.

SALT
Spilling salt is thought to cause an argument that day. To ward off bad luck, people throw a pinch of salt over their left shoulder.

► The 13th day of the month falls on a friday up to three times each year.

QUIZ

1. How many years bad luck is a broken mirror thought to bring?
2. How many witches were thought to meet on a Friday?
3. Why is the number four unlucky in the Far East?

Answers:
1. Seven years 2. 12, and one devil 3. The word for four sounds like the word for death

92 **Unlucky Friday 13th may come from the European belief in witchcraft.** One theory says that Friday was the day that witches held ceremonies to conduct harmful magic. It was said that 12 witches and one devil would meet each Friday, making the number 13 and Friday a doubly unlucky combination.

93 **In China and East Asia there is a superstition called tetraphobia – fear of the number four.** The number is thought to be so unlucky that multistorey buildings are often missing a fourth floor. This superstition has come about because the word for four sounds similar to the word for death in several Far Eastern languages.

94 **People whose careers may involve risk and uncertainty, such as actors, may be superstitious.** There are many superstitions attached to careers in the theatre. Even wishing an actor 'good luck' is unlucky! Instead, it is custom to say 'break a leg'. Another theatre superstition says that a stage should never be left dark. A light, called a 'ghost light', is left on after a performance to keep the ghosts of past performers content.

► Lady Macbeth is the wicked wife in Shakespeare's famous play *Macbeth*. Actors consider it unlucky to speak the name of the play, instead calling it 'the Scottish Play'.

Illusionist magic

95 Illusionist magic involves trickery and skill rather than supernatural powers. It is practised by performance magicians to entertain audiences. These magicians do not pretend to have magical powers, but use their talents to create the illusion of magic.

▲ A classic illusionist's trick is to 'saw a person in half'. During Italian magician Gaetano Trigginao's show *Tablo*, a man is seemingly cut in two.

▲ A well known stage trick involves pulling a rabbit out of a hat.

96 Stage magicians perform magic tricks in theatres and at parties. Typical stage tricks include making objects appear apparently from nowhere, such as pulling a coin from a person's ear. Or the magician might transform objects, for example, turning a white handkerchief red.

97 Escapology is the art of escaping from restraints such as ropes, chains and handcuffs in death-defying stunts. In the early 1900s, American Harry Houdini made daring escapes using just skill and flexibility. He learnt how to pick locks and he could dislocate his shoulders to narrow his body to help him escape.

▼ Escapologist Harry Houdini became known as 'The Handcuff King' because of his incredible ability to free himself.

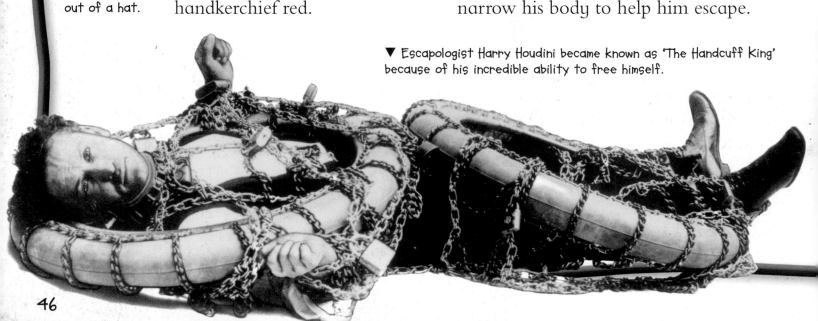

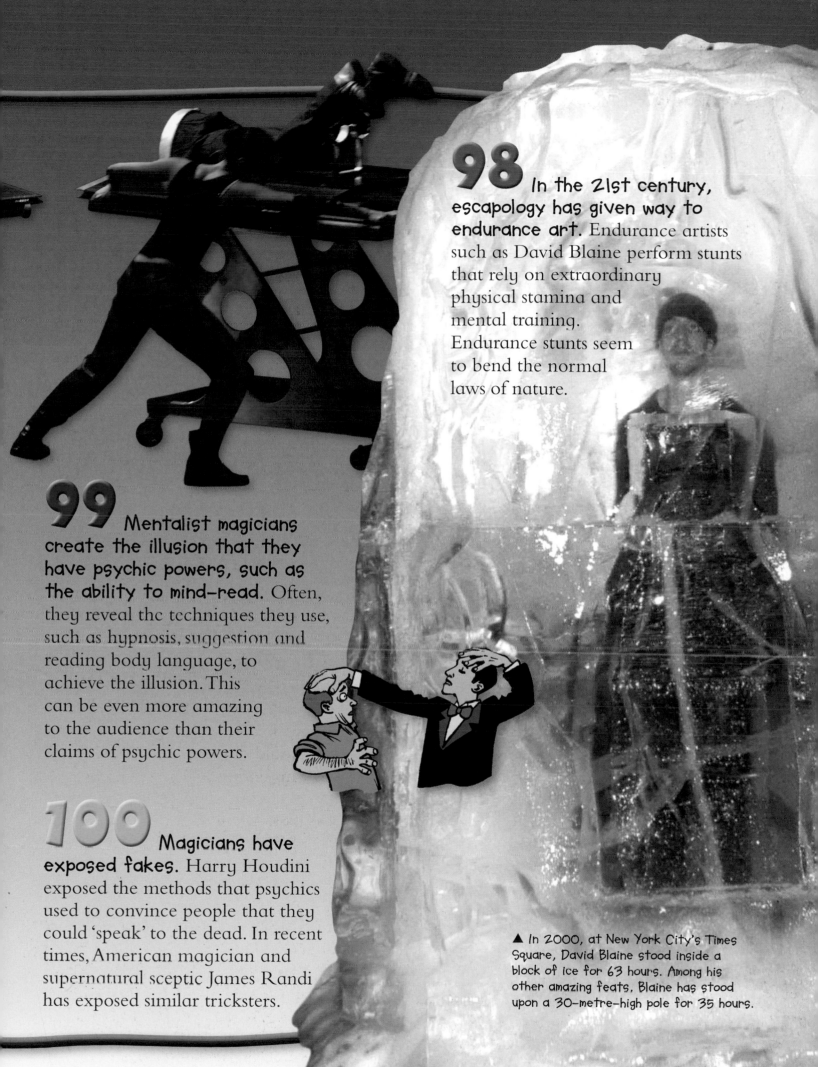

98 In the 21st century, escapology has given way to endurance art. Endurance artists such as David Blaine perform stunts that rely on extraordinary physical stamina and mental training. Endurance stunts seem to bend the normal laws of nature.

99 Mentalist magicians create the illusion that they have psychic powers, such as the ability to mind-read. Often, they reveal the techniques they use, such as hypnosis, suggestion and reading body language, to achieve the illusion. This can be even more amazing to the audience than their claims of psychic powers.

100 Magicians have exposed fakes. Harry Houdini exposed the methods that psychics used to convince people that they could 'speak' to the dead. In recent times, American magician and supernatural sceptic James Randi has exposed similar tricksters.

▲ In 2000, at New York City's Times Square, David Blaine stood inside a block of ice for 63 hours. Among his other amazing feats, Blaine has stood upon a 30-metre-high pole for 35 hours.

Index

Entries in **bold** refer to main subject entries. Entries in *italics* refer to illustrations.

A
alchemy **14–15**, 37
amulets **32**, *32*, 41
animals **26–27**, **43**, *43*
Aristotle 14
astrology 9, **10**, *11*, 37, *42*
augury *16*

B
Baba Yaga **36**
Blaine, David 47, *47*
brownies **39**

C
cats 26, *26*, 27, 44
cave paintings **8**, *8*
circles **35**
crosses 34
Cunning Folk **28**

D
daemons **12**, *12*
dance *9*, 28
Day of the Dead **19**, *19*
Dee, John **37**, *37*
Democritus 29
demons 34, 35
devil 22, 34, 45
divination **10**, 11, *11*, **16–17**, *17*, 34
dolls 22, *22*
dowser *11*
dragons **26**, *26*, 42
druids 30

E
eclipses **42**, *42*
Elixir of Life **21**
elves **38**, *38*
escapology **46**, *46*, 47
'evil eye' **23**, *23*, 32
evil spirits 23, 31, 33

F
fairies **38**, *38*, 39, 42
familiars **26**, *26*
fortune-telling **9**, 16
Fountain of Youth 41
Friday 13th **45**

G
Gandalf the White 7, *7*
Glastonbury Tor, England **24**, *25*
grimoires 22

H
healing 9, *9*, 13, **28–29**
herbalism 28, *28*
hex signs **35**, *35*
hieroglyphs **34**, *34*
high magic 10, **11**, 35
horoscopes *11*, 37
horses 27
horseshoes **33**, *33*
Houdini, Harry 46, *46*, 47

I
illusion 9, *9*, **46–47**
imitative magic **21**
immortality 20, 21, *21*

L
levitation *9*
ley lines 24
luck 6, 44
lucky charms 33

M
magic-makers 6, 11, **36–37**
Magnus, Albertus **37**
Magus, Simon 36
mandrake root **31**, *31*
May Eve 19
medicinal plants 28, *28*, *29*, 30, *30*
Merlin **36**, *36*
metal-working 33
mind-reading 47
mirrors **44**

mistletoe **30**, *31*
mummy's curse **43**
mushrooms **31**

N
Narnia **40**, *40*
Nazca Lines, Peru **25**, *25*
Neverland **41**

O
ojo **23**
omens *42*
oracle **16**, *16*
oracle bones 17, *17*

P
palmistry **17**, *17*
pellars 19
pentagram **34**, *34*
Philosopher's Stone **14**
plants 28, **30–31**
potions *18*, 20, *21*, 23, 31
Potter, Harry **37**, *37*, *38*
priestess 16, *16*

R
rain dance 20, *20*
rainbows 8, *8*
religion 6, 36
rings **33**, *33*
rowan **31**, *31*
rune stones 34

S
Saint Columba **27**
science 8, 15, 37
shadows **22**, *22*
Shakespeare, William 18, 45
shamans 9, *9*, 11, **13**, *13*, **28**, *28*
Socrates 12, *12*
sorcerers 23, 36
spells **10**, *10*, 11, **18–19**, 20, 28, 41, 42
spirit ancestors 24

stone circles **24**, *24*
supernatural beings 6, 22, 25
superstitions **44–45**

T
tea-leaf reading **17**
trolls **38**
Tutankhamun 43, *43*

U
Uluru, Australia **24**, *25*
underworld 25, 41
unicorn **27**, *27*, 29

W
wand **32**, *32*
witches 9, 11, 12, **13**, *13*, *18*, 19, 23, 26, *26*, 31, 32, 33, 36, 45
witchcraft 8, 12, **13**, *13*, 28
witchetty grubs 21, *21*
Wolsey, Cardinal 33

100 facts
Magic & Mystery

NIGHT
SKY

NIG
SKY

LIGHT

GILES SPARROW

SCHOLASTIC discover more™

How to discover more

This book is simple to use and enjoy, but knowing a little bit about how it works will help you discover more about the night sky and what interests you most about it.
Have a great read!

How the pages work

The book is divided into chapters, such as **Watching the night sky**. Each chapter is made up of stand-alone spreads (double pages) that focus on specific topics.

What you can see
Use these panels as guides to spotting objects in the night sky yourself. Each panel shows you what to look for.

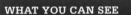

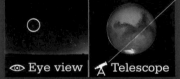

WHAT YOU CAN SEE

👁 Eye view   🔭 Telescope

Viewing notes
Mars has a distinctive red colour. It changes in brightness as our distance from it changes. Amateur telescopes can show dark and light patches on its surface.

Viewing icons
Discover how you can see things differently with your naked eye, binoculars, or a telescope.

Viewing notes
These notes tell you the features to look out for, such as the brightness, colour, and size of a planet.

Introduction
Most spreads have a general introduction to the subject.

Fantastic facts
BIG text gives an amazing fact or quote!

Telescopes [Zooming in]

Use a telescope to view spectacular objects in the night sky, such as stars, planets, and even galaxies! Telescopes brighten and enlarge objects, so we can see much more with them than with the naked eye.

Galileo Galilei
By pointing a telescope at the night sky in the early 1600s, Galileo discovered that planets are round, that the Moon has mountains, and that the Sun, not Earth, is the centre of the solar system.

Galileo Galilei
Italian astronomer Galileo used a telescope to show that Earth orbits the Sun.

Reflecting telescope
The reflecting telescope was invented by English scientist Isaac Newton around 1668. It collects light and bounces it towards an eyepiece lens to create a magnified image.

Viewfinder
This is used to point the larger telescope in the right direction.

How it works
Light enters the telescope through a plate. The rays hit the primary mirror and are reflected to the secondary mirror. This mirror reflects the light back to the eyepiece, where the image is magnified and sent to the eye.

Light enters
Plate

Galileo's telescope
magnified by only 3 times!

Secondary mirror
A smaller mirror reflects light back to the eyepiece.

Light enters

Eyepiece lens
A magnified image is created through this lens.

Primary mirror
This curved mirror collects light.

Refractor telescope
Lens-based telescopes are called refractors. They use lenses to refract (bend) light, directing it towards the eyepiece.

Viewfinder

How it works
Light enters through a large curved lens (called an objective lens) at the front of the telescope. Light rays meet at a point called the focus. As the rays spread apart again, the eyepiece collects them and magnifies an image.

Objective lens

Binoculars
Binoculars are like two small telescopes joined together. They are a good tool for beginner astronomers.

Tripod stand

Binoculars
Although they are not as powerful as a telescope, binoculars are portable and easy to use.

Focus

Eyepiece
The eyepiece forms a magnified image.

Invisible light
Light is a type of radiation (energy travelling through space). Many objects create radiation with more or less energy than visible light has. We can detect it using special telescopes.

VISIBLE LIGHT

X-RAYS

RADIO WAVES

COMBINED VIEW

Four views of Centaurus A
The galaxy Centaurus A is shown in visible light, as an X-ray, and as a radio-wave image. At bottom, all three images are combined.

Digital companion book

Download your free, all-new digital book:

Light-Up Zodiac

Log on to
www.scholastic.com/ discovermore

Enter your unique code:
RXWGHPHNN62T

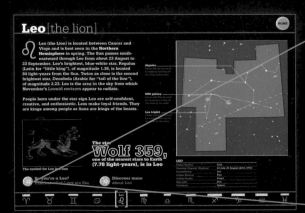

Features a star chart for every zodiac constellation.

Click to find out about people with your sign.

Warning boxes

Follow these guidelines to make sure that you don't damage your eyes when viewing the sky.

WARNING! Use telescopes and binoculars to look at the sky only at night. Never point them directly at the Sun.

18/19
WATCHING THE NIGHT SKY

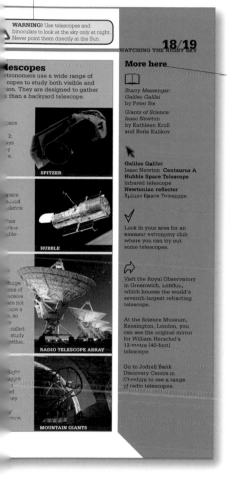

...escopes

...tronomers use a wide range of ...copes to study both visible and ...ion. They are designed to gather ... than a backyard telescope.

SPITZER

HUBBLE

RADIO TELESCOPE ARRAY

MOUNTAIN GIANTS

More here

Starry Messenger: Galileo Galilei by Peter Sis

Giants of Science: Isaac Newton by Kathleen Krull and Boris Kulikov

Galileo Galilei
Isaac Newton **Centaurus A**
Hubble Space Telescope
infrared telescope
Newtonian reflector
Spitzer Space Telescope

Look in your area for an amateur astronomy club where you can try out some telescopes.

Visit the Royal Observatory in Greenwich, London, which houses the world's seventh-largest refracting telescope.

At the Science Museum, Kensington, London, you can see the original mirror for William Herschel's 12-metre (40-foot) telescope.

Go to Jodrell Bank Discovery Centre in Cheshire to see a range of radio telescopes.

Spread types

Look out for different kinds of spreads. Constellation spreads include charts to help you spot groups of stars. Feature spreads on planets, the Moon, the Sun, and galaxies show more objects to look for and how the Universe works.

More here columns

This feature suggests books to read, words to look up on the Internet, places to visit, and things to do.

Key to symbols in **More here** columns

Suggested reading

Do

Keywords for web searches

Places to visit

View from afar

Watch

Mini-glossary

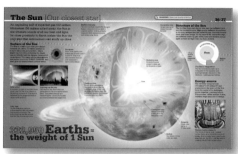

CONSTELLATION SPREAD

Discover the stories and unique stars of each of the major constellations. Use the charts to find star patterns in the sky.

FEATURE SPREAD

Feature spreads have detailed artwork and graphics, as well as fun and amazing facts.

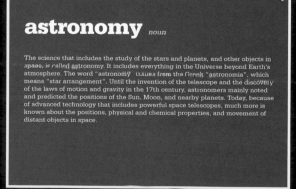

PHOTOGRAPHIC SPREAD

This type of spread focuses on an extraordinary subject and includes images from NASA and the Hubble Space Telescope.

Glossary and index

The glossary explains words and phrases that might not be explained fully on the spreads or in the **More here** columns. The index can help you find pages throughout the book on which words and topics appear.

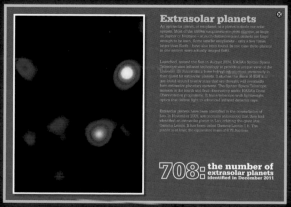

Extrasolar planets

708: the number of extrasolar planets identified in December 2011

Read in-depth night sky encyclopedia entries.

astronomy *noun*

The science that includes the study of the stars and planets, and other objects in space, is called astronomy. It includes everything in the Universe beyond Earth's atmosphere. The word "astronomy" comes from the Greek "astronomia", which means "star arrangement". Until the invention of the telescope and the discovery of the laws of motion and gravity in the 17th century, astronomers mainly noted and predicted the positions of the Sun, Moon, and nearby planets. Today, because of advanced technology that includes powerful space telescopes, much more is known about the positions, physical and chemical properties, and movement of distant objects in space.

Look up night sky words.

Project editor: Dawn Bates

Project art editors: Emma Forge, Tom Forge

Art director: Bryn Walls

Managing editor: Miranda Smith

Illustration: Tim Brown/Pikaia Imaging,
Tim Loughhead/Precision Illustration

Cover designer: Natalie Godwin

DTP: John Goldsmid

Visual content editor: Dwayne Howard

**Executive Director of Photography,
Scholastic:** Steve Diamond

**"Anyone who does not ... gaze
up and see the wonder ... of a dark
night sky
filled with countless stars loses
a sense of their fundamental
connectedness to the Universe."**
—DR BRIAN GREENE, COLUMBIA UNIVERSITY PHYSICIST

Library of Congress Cataloging-in-Publication Data Available
Distributed in the UK by Scholastic UK Ltd, Westfield Road, Southam
Warwickshire, England CV47 0RA

ISBN 978-1-407-13157-3

10 9 8 7 6 5 4 3 2 1   12 13 14 15 16

Printed in Singapore   46
First edition, May 2012

Contents

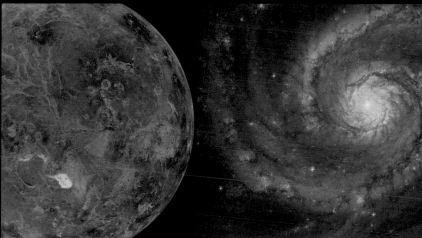

Watching the night sky

Watch the sky	14
Seeing more	16
Telescopes	18
View from Earth	20
Constellations	22
Northern skies	24
Southern skies	26
Equatorial skies	28
Meteors	32

Searching for the stars

The Sun	36
Variety of stars	38
Orion	40
Sagittarius	42
Celestial fireworks	44
Leo	46
How far?	48
Cygnus	50
Scorpius	52
Lyra	56
Taurus	58
Strange stars	60

Discovering amazing planets

The planets	64
Orbiting the Sun	66
Earth's Moon	68
Moon map	70
The Moon	72
Mercury and Venus	76
Mars	78
Jupiter	80
Saturn's rings	82
Outer planets	84
Moons	86
Flying objects	88

Galaxies and the Universe

Our galaxy	92
Cloud galaxies	96
Andromeda	98
Galaxies galore	100
To the edge	104
Glossary	106
Index	109
Credits and acknowledgments	112

Northern lights

The breathtaking northern lights thrill sky watchers near Arctic regions. Often called the aurora borealis, this natural light display is created when solar wind particles (see page 36) collide with Earth's atmosphere. The resulting vibrant colours dance across the sky.

Galaxy crash

Galaxies are so big and have so much
gravitational pull that they can cluster
together and collide. This group of five
galaxies (two galaxies have merged to
look like one) is called Stephan's Quintet.
Although the bluish galaxy appears to
be on a collision course with the others,
in reality it is much closer to Earth.

Watchi
nigh

- Why do the stars appear to change position?

* What will next be visible from Earth in 4530?

- What did Galileo discover?

ng the
t sky

The hour just after sunset is a great time to view the night sky. As day turns to night, you can see all kinds of objects with your naked eye, from nearby planets to distant stars.

Light pollution

As humans switch on electric lights after sunset, faint stars become hard to see. For the best sky views, try to get away from artificial lights, or block them out by positioning yourself behind a building.

Urban light
Electric lights can flood the night sky with artificial brightness.

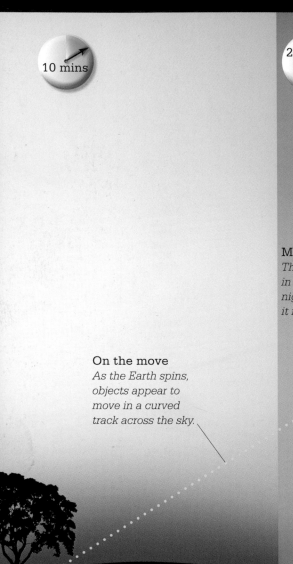

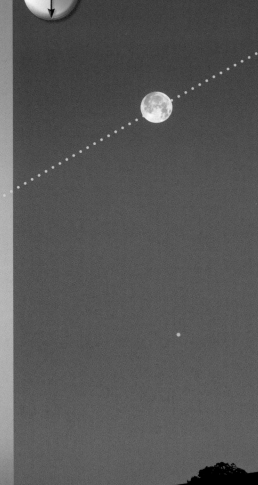

10 mins

20 mins

30 mins

Moon rising
The Moon's location in the sky changes nightly. At Full Moon, it rises as the Sun sets.

On the move
As the Earth spins, objects appear to move in a curved track across the sky.

Earth's shadow

Turn away from the sunset and look at the opposite side of the sky, just above the horizon. See a curved band of darkness beginning to rise? It's Earth's shadow, cast on the atmosphere.

Rising Moon

Around the time of the Full Moon (see page 69), the Moon will be rising as the Sun sets. The Moon's light is a faint reflection of the Sun's, but at night it becomes the brightest object in the sky.

Planet spotting

Venus, Mars, and Jupiter can all outshine the brightest stars. They may be the first starlike objects visible after sunset. You can tell a planet from a star because a planet does not twinkle.

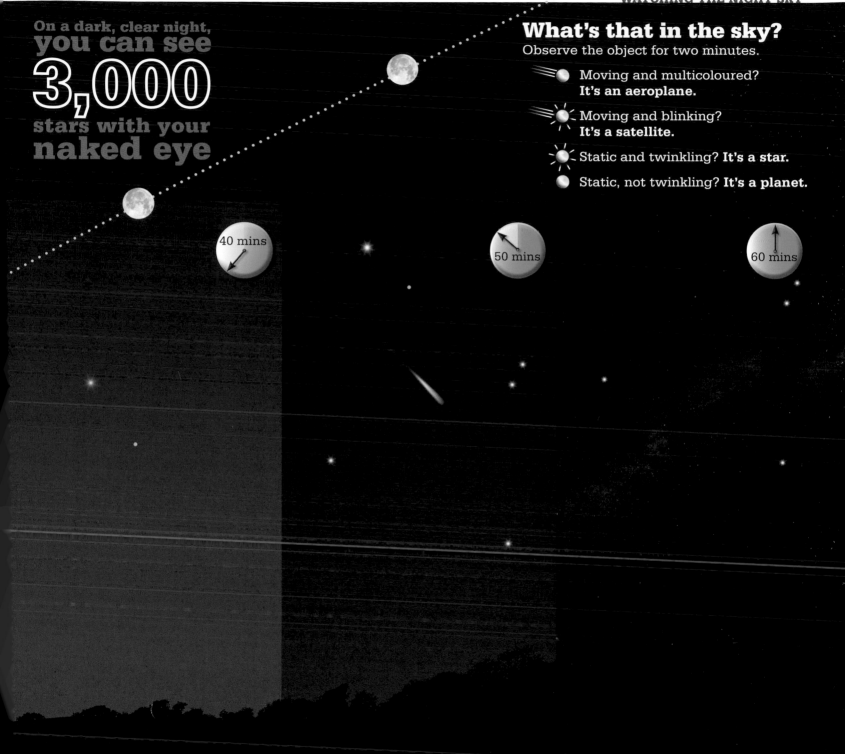

On a dark, clear night,
you can see
3,000
stars with your
naked eye

What's that in the sky?
Observe the object for two minutes.

Moving and multicoloured?
It's an aeroplane.

Moving and blinking?
It's a satellite.

Static and twinkling? **It's a star.**

Static, not twinkling? **It's a planet.**

40 mins

50 mins

60 mins

First stars
Eventually, the sky will be
dark enough for the first stars
to appear. They may twinkle and
flicker as their light is bent and
warped on its journey through
Earth's turbulent air.

Shooting star
As the sky gets darker, you may see
a streak of light. This is a meteor, or
shooting star (see pages 32–33), a
fragment of rock that burns up in
a blaze of heat and light as it plunges
from space into Earth's atmosphere.

The Milky Way
In full darkness, you can see a pale
band of light – the Milky Way (see
pages 94–95). By the end of the
hour, it appears that the Moon and
stars have moved, but in fact the
Earth has spun beneath them.

You can see thousands of stars, and even some details on the Moon, with just your naked eye. To see farther and in greater focus, you will need binoculars or a telescope. An object's magnitude, or brightness, determines its visibility.

You can see an object up to **2.5 million light-years away with the naked eye**

Naked eye
With your eyes alone, you can see details on the Moon, nearby or especially bright stars, and even the closest galaxies.

What you can see
Faintest object visible is of magnitude 6 (see opposite page).

Naked-eye view of the Moon
You can make out vague dark and light patches.

Binoculars
Binoculars (see page 18) collect more light than your eyes do, so they can help you see fainter objects. They also magnify things so that you can see them in more detail.

What you can see
Faintest object visible is of magnitude 9.

Binocular view of the Moon
The patches form dark, smooth seas and bright, rocky highlands.

Backyard telescope
Telescopes (see pages 18–19) collect even more light than binoculars do, revealing the faintest objects and showing highly magnified, detailed images.

What you can see
Faintest object visible with a small telescope is around magnitude 12.

Telescopic view of the Moon
Through a telescope, you can see that the Moon is covered in mountains, craters (like this one), and smooth lava plains.

Try this!
To see faint objects with your naked eye, binoculars, or a telescope, use averted vision. Look slightly away from the object and watch it from the more sensitive edges of your eye.

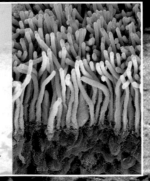

Central vision
The rod cells in the centre of the eye (shown in pale brown, right) are good for colour vision, but not for seeing faint detail.

WARNING! Use telescopes and binoculars to look at the sky only at night. Never point them directly at the Sun.

Use your naked eye to see:

Moon	400,000 km (250,000 miles) away
Saturn	1.5 billion km (900 million miles) away
Pleiades	400 light-years away
Andromeda galaxy	2.5 million light-years away

Pleiades
Many people can see seven stars with their naked eye in this cluster in Taurus (see pages 58–59).

Use your binoculars to see:

Asteroid Ceres	280 million km (175 million miles) away
Moons of Jupiter	600 million km (372 million miles) away
Uranus	2.7 billion km (1.7 billion miles) away
M101 galaxy	25 million light-years away

Jupiter and moons
Binoculars show Jupiter as a tiny disc orbited by the starlike points of its moons.

Use your telescope to see:

Neptune	4.3 billion km (2.7 billion miles) away
Ring Nebula	2,300 light-years away
M87 galaxy	54 million light-years away

Messier 87
This gigantic galaxy, visible with a telescope, contains one trillion stars.

Photographing the sky

A camera can be a great way to see more detail and fainter objects. Long exposures allow cameras to soak up more light than our eyes can, increasing contrast and revealing the colours in starlight.

Seen with the naked eye
The Milky Way appears as an arc of faint white light stretching across the sky.

Seen with long exposure
A photograph can reveal colourful star clouds and the gas and dust between them.

How brightness is measured

Astronomers measure the brightness of objects in the sky on a scale called magnitude. Fainter objects have higher magnitudes. An object that is 1 unit of magnitude lower than another is about 2.5 times brighter.

Magnitude bar
The brighter an object is, the lower its magnitude.

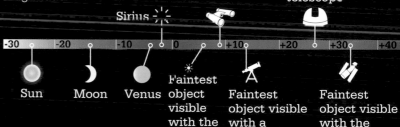

Faintest object visible with binoculars

Faintest object visible with an 8-m (26-foot) telescope

Sirius

-30   -20   -10   0   +10   +20   +30   +40

Sun

Moon

Venus

Faintest object visible with the naked eye

Faintest object visible with a backyard telescope

Faintest object visible with the Hubble Space Telescope

Telescopes [Zooming in]

Use a telescope to view spectacular objects in the night sky, such as stars, planets, and even galaxies! Telescopes brighten and enlarge objects, so we can see much more with them than with the naked eye.

Galileo Galilei

By pointing a telescope at the night sky in the early 1600s, Galileo discovered that planets are round, that the Moon has mountains, and that the Sun, not Earth, is the centre of the solar system.

Galileo Galilei
Italian astronomer Galileo used a telescope to show that Earth orbits the Sun.

Reflecting telescope

The reflecting telescope was invented by English scientist Isaac Newton around 1668. It collects light and bounces it towards an eyepiece lens to create a magnified image.

Viewfinder
This is used to point the larger telescope in the right direction.

How it works
Light enters the telescope through a plate. The rays hit the primary mirror and are reflected to the secondary mirror. This mirror reflects the light back to the eyepiece, where the image is magnified and sent to the eye.

Eyepiece lens
A magnified image is created through this lens.

Primary mirror
This curved mirror collects light.

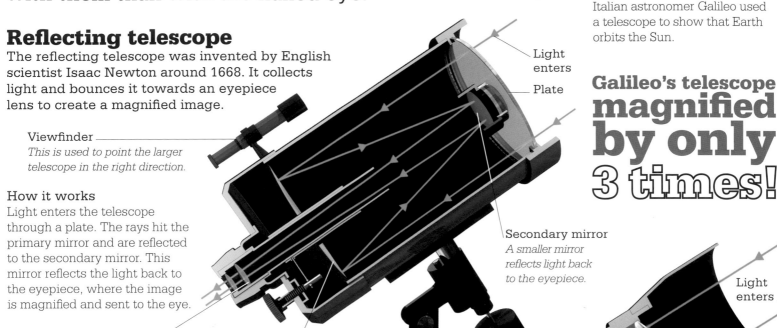

Light enters

Plate

Secondary mirror
A smaller mirror reflects light back to the eyepiece.

Galileo's telescope magnified by only 3 times!

Refractor telescope

Lens-based telescopes are called refractors. They use lenses to refract (bend) light, directing it towards the eyepiece.

How it works
Light enters through a large curved lens (called an objective lens) at the front of the telescope. Light rays meet at a point called the focus. As the rays spread apart again, the eyepiece collects them and magnifies an image.

Viewfinder

Light enters

Objective lens

Binoculars

Binoculars are like two small telescopes joined together. They are a good tool for beginner astronomers.

Tripod stand

Focus

Eyepiece
The eyepiece forms a magnified image.

Binoculars
Although they are not as powerful as a telescope, binoculars are portable and easy to use.

Invisible light

Light is a type of radiation (energy travelling through space). Many objects create radiation with more or less energy than visible light has. We can detect it using special telescopes.

VISIBLE LIGHT

X-RAYS

RADIO WAVES

COMBINED VIEW

Four views of Centaurus A
The galaxy Centaurus A is shown in visible light, as an X-ray, and as a radio-wave image. At bottom, all three images are combined.

Super-telescopes

Professional astronomers use a wide range of high-tech telescopes to study both visible and invisible radiation. They are designed to gather a lot more light than a backyard telescope.

Spitzer
NASA's Spitzer Space Telescope orbits high above Earth. It detects infrared rays that are blocked by Earth's atmosphere.

SPITZER

Hubble
NASA's Hubble Space Telescope is positioned far above the turbulence caused by Earth's atmosphere, so it has a clearer, sharper view than any other visible-light telescope.

HUBBLE

Radio telescope
Radio waves are so large and faint that astronomers build huge receiving dishes, tens of metres across, to receive them. Even these are not big enough to produce a really sharp picture, so radio telescopes are gathered in groups called arrays, designed to study the same object together.

RADIO TELESCOPE ARRAY

Dome telescope
The largest visible-light telescopes can measure 10 metres (33 feet) or more across. Located on mountaintops, they avoid interference from clouds and any atmospheric turbulence.

MOUNTAIN GIANTS

More here

Starry Messenger: Galileo Galilei by Peter Sís

Giants of Science: Isaac Newton by Kathleen Krull and Boris Kulikov

Galileo Galilei
Isaac Newton **Centaurus A**
Hubble Space Telescope
infrared telescope
Newtonian reflector
Spitzer Space Telescope

Look in your area for an amateur astronomy club where you can try out some telescopes.

Visit the Royal Observatory in Greenwich, London, which houses the world's seventh-largest refracting telescope.

At the Science Museum, Kensington, London, you can see the original mirror for William Herschel's 12-metre (40-foot) telescope.

Go to Jodrell Bank Discovery Centre in Cheshire to see a range of radio telescopes.

Looking at the night sky for patterns of stars, called constellations, is a fun and rewarding part of astronomy. One of the most famous constellations in the northern sky is the Great Bear, also called Ursa Major (in Latin). Within its outline is the group of stars known as the Plough.

88 : the official number of **constellations that have been** catalogued by modern **astronomers**

Seven stars
The seven brightest stars of Ursa Major form an asterism, a simple pattern that is smaller than the constellation as a whole.

Large constellation
Ursa Major's fainter stars spread across a large area of sky, making the Great Bear the third-largest constellation.

North and south

Some constellations are easier to identify than others because of their shape. The Great Bear is a complicated shape and takes some imagination (see opposite page). The Southern Cross (Crux Australis) is by contrast an easy shape to spot in a starry sky.

The Great Bear
The pattern of Ursa Major resembles a bear. Parts of its body and tail, shown in yellow, form another pattern, the Plough.

The Southern Cross
The most famous constellation in the southern skies, the Southern Cross is also the smallest constellation of all.

What shape do you see?

While the positions of the stars have barely moved over thousands of years, different cultures have seen the same groups of stars in different ways. The ancient Greeks named 48 constellations, most based on mythological figures. Ancient Egyptian and medieval Arabic astronomers recognized different names and shapes.

The Big Dipper
American stargazers see the seven brightest stars in Ursa Major as a ladle.

The Plough
European stargazers usually compare the same seven stars to an old-fashioned plough.

Celestial globe
This beautiful 1878 globe is decorated with elaborate figures. It illustrates constellations such as Leo, the Lion, and Hydra, the Water Snake.

Leo
This star pattern forms the image of a crouching lion (see pages 46–47).

Hydra
The largest constellation, Hydra, is shown as a water snake.

Sky in reverse
The pictures on this globe are reversed, compared to our view from Earth.

Look for a constellation

The best way to find your way around the sky is to learn a few key star patterns, such as the ones in Chapter 2. Then use the large star maps on pages 24–29 to see how they relate to other constellations and to the entire sky.

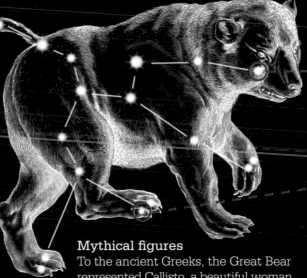

Mizar
The middle star of the bear's tail has a faint nearby companion named Alcor.

Dark skies
To see a constellation clearly, choose a dark night and avoid light pollution (see page 14).

Mythical figures
To the ancient Greeks, the Great Bear represented Callisto, a beautiful woman who was turned into a bear by the jealous goddess Hera.

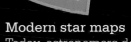

Modern star maps
Today, astronomers define 88 constellations – areas of sky around the traditional patterns. In this system, every object in the sky is placed in a constellation.

Northern skies [Star map]

The northern half of the celestial sphere (see page 20), the region of sky familiar to European and Asian astronomers, was mapped with many constellations long ago. They are positioned around the north celestial pole, marked by the star Polaris.

NORTHERN HEMISPHERE

Northern Hemisphere

This map shows the sky as it appears if you stand at the North Pole looking straight up. These stars can be seen at various times of year from the Northern Hemisphere. But if you are south of the Equator, the stars that are closest to the North Pole are always out of sight.

Stars and other objects

This map shows all the stars visible to the naked eye in this part of the sky, as well as some bright and interesting deep-sky objects – star clusters, gaseous nebulae, and galaxies.

A different view

The constellations on the big chart come mostly from a list of 48 star patterns written down by European astronomers in the second century CE. Chinese astronomers saw the sky differently, and created constellations out of smaller groups of stars.

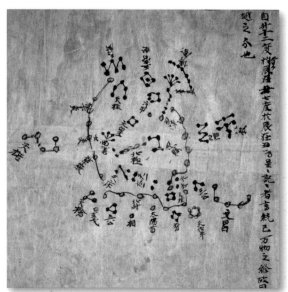

Ancient Chinese map
This map from around 650 CE shows a Chinese astronomer's view of star patterns in the Northern Hemisphere.

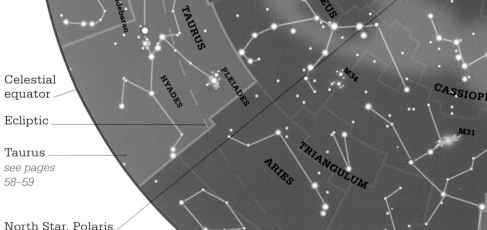

Leo
see pages 46–47

North Pole

Orion
see pages 40–41

Celestial equator

Ecliptic

Taurus
see pages 58–59

North Star, Polaris

SEXTANS

LEO

CANCER

LEO MINOR

THE PLOUGH

CANIS MINOR

Procyon

GEMINI

LYNX

MONOCEROS

Betelgeuse

M35

AURIGA

M36

M38

Capella

CAMELOPARDALIS

Polaris

PERSEUS

ORION

Aldebaran

TAURUS

HYADES

PLEIADES

M34

CASSIOPEIA

M31

TRIANGULUM

ARIES

CETUS

PISCES

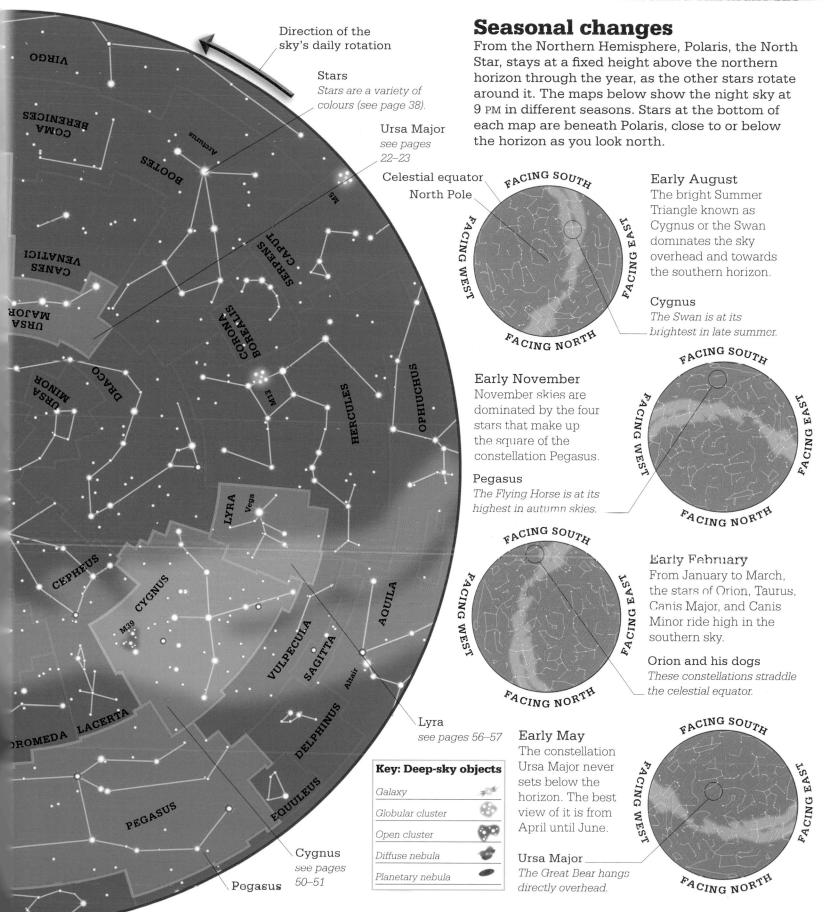

Direction of the sky's daily rotation

Stars
Stars are a variety of colours (see page 38).

Ursa Major
see pages 22–23

Celestial equator
North Pole

Lyra
see pages 56–57

Cygnus
see pages 50–51

Pegasus

VIRGO
COMA BERENICES
BOOTES
Arcturus
CANES VENATICI
URSA MAJOR
SERPENS CAPUT
CORONA BOREALIS
M5
M13
HERCULES
OPHIUCHUS
URSA MINOR
DRACO
CEPHEUS
LYRA *Vega*
CYGNUS
M39
AQUILA
VULPECULA
SAGITTA
Altair
DELPHINUS
LACERTA
ANDROMEDA
EQUULEUS
PEGASUS

Key: Deep-sky objects

Galaxy	
Globular cluster	
Open cluster	
Diffuse nebula	
Planetary nebula	

Seasonal changes

From the Northern Hemisphere, Polaris, the North Star, stays at a fixed height above the northern horizon through the year, as the other stars rotate around it. The maps below show the night sky at 9 PM in different seasons. Stars at the bottom of each map are beneath Polaris, close to or below the horizon as you look north.

FACING SOUTH
FACING WEST
FACING EAST
FACING NORTH

Early August
The bright Summer Triangle known as Cygnus or the Swan dominates the sky overhead and towards the southern horizon.

Cygnus
The Swan is at its brightest in late summer.

FACING SOUTH
FACING WEST
FACING EAST
FACING NORTH

Early November
November skies are dominated by the four stars that make up the square of the constellation Pegasus.

Pegasus
The Flying Horse is at its highest in autumn skies.

FACING SOUTH
FACING WEST
FACING EAST
FACING NORTH

Early February
From January to March, the stars of Orion, Taurus, Canis Major, and Canis Minor ride high in the southern sky.

Orion and his dogs
These constellations straddle the celestial equator.

FACING SOUTH
FACING WEST
FACING EAST
FACING NORTH

Early May
The constellation Ursa Major never sets below the horizon. The best view of it is from April until June.

Ursa Major
The Great Bear hangs directly overhead.

Southern skies [Star map]

The constellations that lie to the south of the celestial equator (see page 28) have a wide range of ages, sizes, and brightnesses. Some of them are the most brilliant in the sky, while others – particularly those around the south celestial pole – are the most obscure.

SOUTHERN HEMISPHERE

What you can see

This map shows the sky as it would appear if you stood at the South Pole and looked straight up. Many of these stars are also visible from the Northern Hemisphere, but the farther north you go, the farther the south celestial pole sinks out of sight.

Mapping the sky
This map shows all the stars visible to the naked eye in this part of the sky, as well as some bright and interesting deep-sky objects – star clusters, nebulae, and galaxies.

Southern figures
The constellations of the Southern Hemisphere depict a variety of mythical figures, animals, tools, and inventions.

Discovering constellations

Parts of the southern sky closest to the celestial equator were known to the ancient Greeks and included in their original list of 48 constellations. It was the 1500s, however, before the first European sailors saw the sky around the south celestial pole.

Nicolas Louis de Lacaille
This French astronomer catalogued nearly 10,000 southern stars in the 1750s. He named 14 new constellations in the process.

Centaurus

Scorpius
see pages 52–53

Crux

Celestial equator

Ecliptic

Sagittarius
see pages 42–43

No South Star
Unlike in the Northern Hemisphere, there is no bright star close to the south celestial pole.

VIRGO · CORVUS · Spica · CENTAURUS · LIBRA · LUPUS · OPHIUCHUS · M4 · Antares · SCORPIUS · M6 · SERPENS CAUDA · M7 · M20 · M24 · M25 · SCUTUM · M28 · M22 · M11 · SAGITTARIUS · CORONA AUSTRALIS · NORMA · CIRCINUS · Alpha Centauri · CRUX · Acrux · TRIANGULUM AUSTRALE · ARA · TELESCOPIUM · PAVO · APUS · MUSCA · OCTANS · SMC · TUCANA · INDUS · MICROSCOPIUM · CAPRICORNUS · AQUILA · GRUS · PISCIS AUSTRINUS · Fomalhaut · AQUARIUS

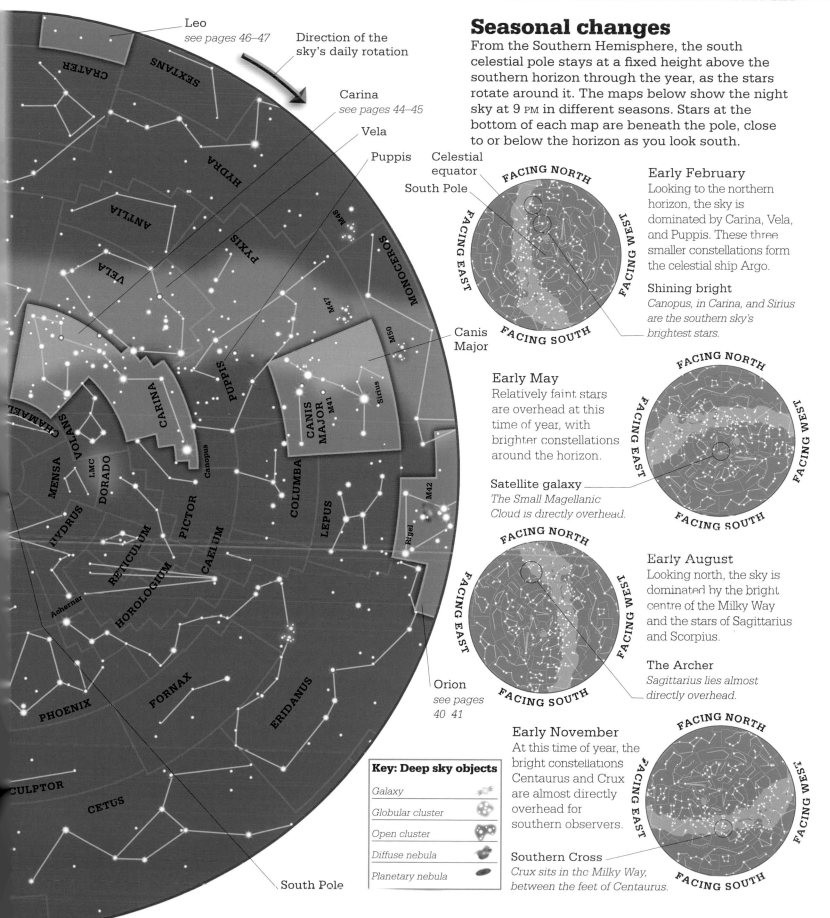

Leo
see pages 46–47

Direction of the sky's daily rotation

Carina
see pages 44–45

Vela

Puppis

Celestial equator

South Pole

CRATER

SEXTANS

HYDRA

ANTLIA

VELA

PYXIS

MONOCEROS

Canis Major

CARINA

PUPPIS

CANIS MAJOR

M47

M50

M48

Sirius

M41

CHAMAELEON

MENSA

VOLANS

LMC

DORADO

HYDRUS

RETICULUM

PICTOR

CAELUM

COLUMBA

LEPUS

Canopus

Rigel

M42

Orion
see pages 40–41

Achernar

HOROLOGIUM

PHOENIX

FORNAX

ERIDANUS

SCULPTOR

CETUS

South Pole

Key: Deep sky objects

Galaxy	
Globular cluster	
Open cluster	
Diffuse nebula	
Planetary nebula	

Seasonal changes

From the Southern Hemisphere, the south celestial pole stays at a fixed height above the southern horizon through the year, as the stars rotate around it. The maps below show the night sky at 9 PM in different seasons. Stars at the bottom of each map are beneath the pole, close to or below the horizon as you look south.

FACING NORTH

FACING WEST

FACING EAST

FACING SOUTH

Early February

Looking to the northern horizon, the sky is dominated by Carina, Vela, and Puppis. These three smaller constellations form the celestial ship Argo.

Shining bright

Canopus, in Carina, and Sirius are the southern sky's brightest stars.

FACING NORTH

FACING WEST

FACING EAST

FACING SOUTH

Early May

Relatively faint stars are overhead at this time of year, with brighter constellations around the horizon.

Satellite galaxy

The Small Magellanic Cloud is directly overhead.

FACING NORTH

FACING WEST

FACING EAST

FACING SOUTH

Early August

Looking north, the sky is dominated by the bright centre of the Milky Way and the stars of Sagittarius and Scorpius.

The Archer

Sagittarius lies almost directly overhead.

FACING NORTH

FACING WEST

FACING EAST

FACING SOUTH

Early November

At this time of year, the bright constellations Centaurus and Crux are almost directly overhead for southern observers.

Southern Cross

Crux sits in the Milky Way, between the feet of Centaurus.

Equatorial skies [Star map]

The sky map is divided equally into northern and southern hemispheres by the celestial equator. Around the equator are the 12 zodiac constellations, which some people relate to their birthdays.

View of both hemispheres

Except at the poles, stargazers in one hemisphere can always see some stars in the other hemisphere. The closer to the Equator you are, the more of the other hemisphere's stars you can see.

EQUATORIAL SKIES

Star map
This map shows the stars around the celestial equator, visible from both hemispheres.

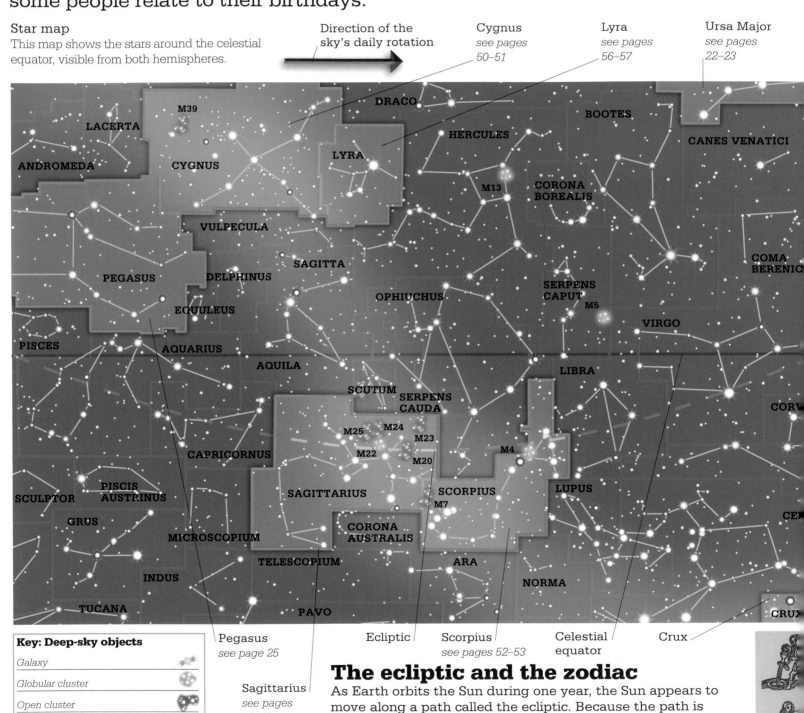

Direction of the sky's daily rotation

Cygnus
see pages 50–51

Lyra
see pages 56–57

Ursa Major
see pages 22–23

DRACO
BOOTES
M39
LACERTA
HERCULES
CANES VENATICI
ANDROMEDA
CYGNUS
LYRA
M13
CORONA BOREALIS
VULPECULA
COMA BERENIC
SAGITTA
PEGASUS
DELPHINUS
SERPENS CAPUT
M5
OPHIUCHUS
EQUULEUS
VIRGO
PISCES
AQUARIUS
AQUILA
LIBRA
SCUTUM
CORV
SERPENS CAUDA
M25 M24
M23
M22 M20
M4
CAPRICORNUS
SCORPIUS
LUPUS
PISCIS AUSTRINUS
SAGITTARIUS
M7
CE
SCULPTOR
GRUS
MICROSCOPIUM
CORONA AUSTRALIS
ARA
INDUS
TELESCOPIUM
NORMA
TUCANA
PAVO
CRUX

Key: Deep-sky objects

Galaxy	
Globular cluster	
Open cluster	
Diffuse nebula	
Planetary nebula	

Pegasus
see page 25

Sagittarius
see pages 42–43

Ecliptic

Scorpius
see pages 52–53

Celestial equator

Crux

The ecliptic and the zodiac

As Earth orbits the Sun during one year, the Sun appears to move along a path called the ecliptic. Because the path is tilted at an angle, the Sun spends six months north and south of the celestial equator. The 12 major constellations that the Sun passes through each year form a band called the zodiac.

Mapping the skies

The earliest star charts and catalogues date from ancient Iraq, around 1200 BCE. Many of these were passed on to Greek astronomers such as Ptolemy, who wrote a summary of ancient astronomy called the *Almagest* around 150 CE.

Ptolemy (ca. 100–170 CE)
His *Almagest* includes a list of 48 constellations of northern and equatorial skies.

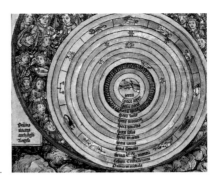

Ptolemaic universe
Ptolemy believed that the Earth was the centre of the Universe, with the Sun, Moon, planets, and stars circling around it.

Leo
see pages 46–47

Canis Minor
see page 40

Orion
see pages 40–41

Taurus
see pages 58–59

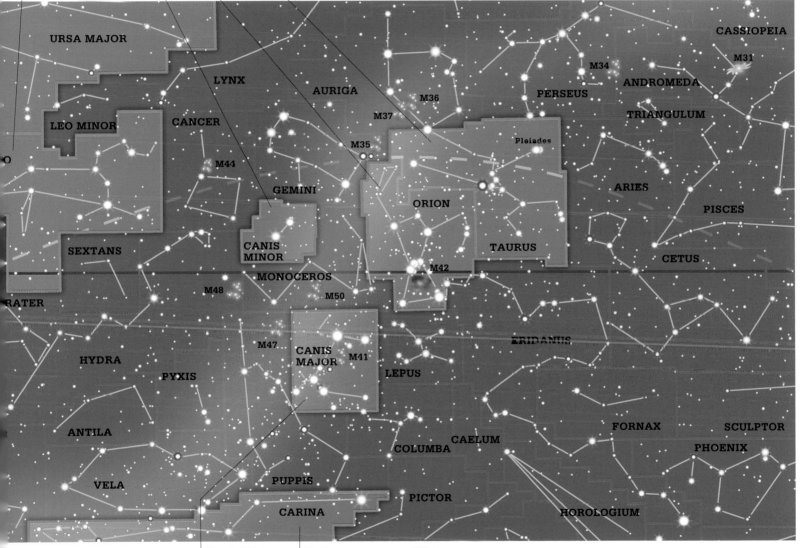

CASSIOPEIA
M31
URSA MAJOR
M34
LYNX
ANDROMEDA
AURIGA
M36
PERSEUS
TRIANGULUM
M37
LEO MINOR
CANCER
M35
Pleiades
M44
ARIES
GEMINI
ORION
PISCES
SEXTANS
CANIS MINOR
TAURUS
CETUS
MONOCEROS
M42
M48
M50
ERIDANUS
M47
CANIS MAJOR
M41
HYDRA
PYXIS
LEPUS
ANTILA
CAELUM
FORNAX
SCULPTOR
COLUMBA
PHOENIX
VELA
PUPPIS
PICTOR
HOROLOGIUM
CARINA
CRATER
O

Canis Major
see page 40

Carina
see pages 44–45

Signs of the zodiac
Whichever constellation the Sun is in at the time you are born is called your zodiac sign. Some people believe that your sign can influence your personality.

The 13th sign of the zodiac?
Each December, the Sun spends 18 days in the constellation of Ophiuchus, the Serpent Bearer, but Ophiuchus isn't counted as an official zodiac sign.

Hale-Bopp over Hawaii

Comets are chunks of rock and ice that orbit the Sun. A rise in temperature as they approach the Sun triggers activity. In 1997, the stunning Hale-Bopp, shown here streaking above the clouds over Hawaii, was one of the brightest comets ever seen. It was visible for several months and will next be seen from Earth in 4530.

Meteors [Shooting stars]

Watch the sky on a clear night, and you might spot a fast-moving streak across the darkness. It could be a meteor, commonly known as a shooting star, created as space debris burns up in the atmosphere.

Meteor shower
Dozens or even hundreds of shooting stars per hour appear to come from the same part of the sky during a meteor shower. The heaviest showers, with thousands of meteors per hour, are called meteor storms.

A link to comets
Giovanni Schiaparelli, a 19th-century astronomer, realized that meteor streams are spread out along the orbits of comets. He concluded that meteor showers are produced when comets decay.

Giovanni Schiaparelli
This Italian astronomer discovered the link between meteors and comets.

Meteorites
Among the dust and debris of the solar system are bigger chunks of rock. Those that are large enough to travel through Earth's atmosphere without burning up are called meteorites once they reach Earth's surface. Meteorites range in size from rocks only a few centimetres long to rare asteroids (see page 88) that can be many kilometres wide.

Landing on Earth
This meteorite landed in Canyon Diablo, Arizona, USA.

Life of a meteorite
As a meteor hits Earth's atmosphere, it begins to heat up. Many meteors burn away completely, but the occasional large rock makes it through the atmosphere and slams into Earth's surface, sometimes causing a huge crater. It is now known as a meteorite.

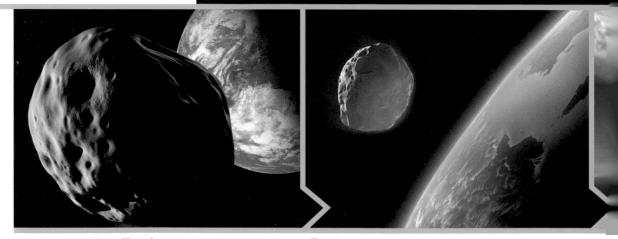

1 Approaching Earth
A meteor may meet our planet head-on at speeds of thousands of kilometres per hour, or catch up with it much more slowly.

2 Entering the atmosphere
Friction with air molecules in the upper atmosphere heats the meteor until it is red hot and starts to glow.

Space junk

Most meteors and meteorites are natural debris left over from the birth of our solar system. But in the past 50 years, human space explorers have been filling space with rubbish, from flecks of paint to broken satellites. Some of that rubbish re-enters the atmosphere and burns up, but a lot hangs around in Earth's orbit.

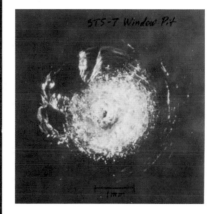

Damage

NASA's space shuttle *Challenger* suffered occasional damage from collisions with fragments of space junk. This hole in its window was made by a fleck of paint.

1,000
tonnes of space debris land on Earth each year

3 **Fireball!**
The largest and brightest meteors are called fireballs. They are most likely to hit Earth.

4 **Impact craters**
Rare meteorites 10 m (30 ft) across or more can gouge craters out of the Earth, but most meteorite impacts are much smaller.

5 **Death of the dinosaurs**
An enormous meteorite impact, 65 million years ago in present-day Mexico, plunged Earth into a climate crisis that may have wiped out the dinosaurs.

Search the S

- Why does the Sun have spots?

* Where in the night sky can you see a horse's head?

- What is a red giant?

ing for
tars

The Sun [Our closest star]

An exploding ball of superhot gas 150 million kilometres (93 million miles) away, the Sun is the ultimate source of all our heat and light. Its close proximity to Earth makes the Sun the only star that astronomers can study up close.

Surface of the Sun

The Sun is a ball of gas that gets denser towards its centre. Its visible surface is a layer called the photosphere, which marks the boundary between the dense, opaque interior and the thinner, transparent outer layers. The gases of the photosphere are heated to around 5,500°C (9,600°F), and they glow an incandescent yellow-white.

Sunspots
Even cooler parts of the surface are around 3,000°C (5,500°F). They look dark because they are cool compared to their surroundings.

Surface features
The Sun's surface constantly changes. Rising columns of hot gas give it a grainy pattern, and its powerful magnetic field creates sunspots and violent solar flares.

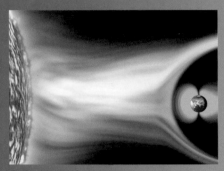

Solar wind
A constant stream of particles blows away from the Sun at hundreds of kilometres per second. This wind is deflected by the magnetic fields of planets such as Earth.

Lighting up the sky
Particles from the Sun's wind are channelled into the atmosphere above Earth. This creates strange and beautiful lights – the aurora borealis and aurora australis (see pages 8–9).

Solar flare
Sudden changes to the Sun's shifting magnetic field can release huge amounts of energy. This energy heats up gas that escapes from the Sun, causing solar flares.

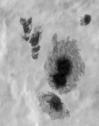

Visible surface
Known as the photosphere, the visible surface of the Sun is actually a layer of mist 1,000 kilometres (600 miles) deep. The surface just appears solid because it is so far away from Earth.

332,950 Earths = the weight of 1 Sun

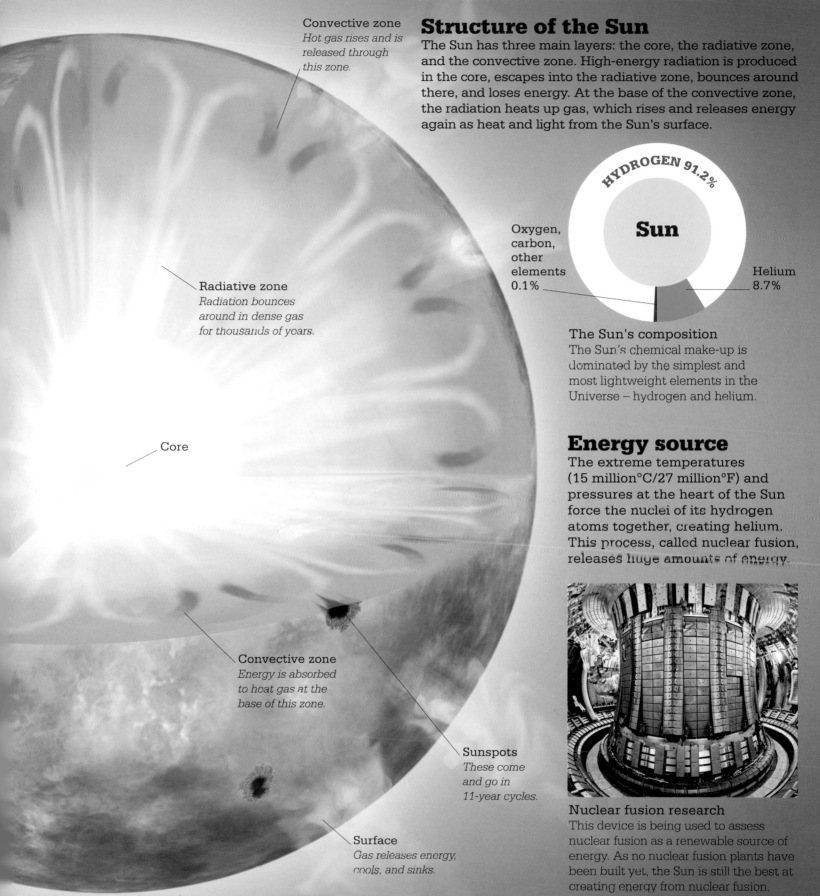

Structure of the Sun

The Sun has three main layers: the core, the radiative zone, and the convective zone. High-energy radiation is produced in the core, escapes into the radiative zone, bounces around there, and loses energy. At the base of the convective zone, the radiation heats up gas, which rises and releases energy again as heat and light from the Sun's surface.

Convective zone
Hot gas rises and is released through this zone.

Radiative zone
Radiation bounces around in dense gas for thousands of years.

Core

Convective zone
Energy is absorbed to heat gas at the base of this zone.

Sunspots
These come and go in 11-year cycles.

Surface
Gas releases energy, cools, and sinks.

HYDROGEN 91.2%

Sun

Oxygen, carbon, other elements 0.1%

Helium 8.7%

The Sun's composition
The Sun's chemical make-up is dominated by the simplest and most lightweight elements in the Universe – hydrogen and helium.

Energy source

The extreme temperatures (15 million°C/27 million°F) and pressures at the heart of the Sun force the nuclei of its hydrogen atoms together, creating helium. This process, called nuclear fusion, releases huge amounts of energy.

Nuclear fusion research
This device is being used to assess nuclear fusion as a renewable source of energy. As no nuclear fusion plants have been built yet, the Sun is still the best at creating energy from nuclear fusion.

Variety of stars [So colourful]

A careful look at the night sky reveals a huge range in the colours and brightness of stars. How are stars formed, and what causes the differences between them?

Multicoloured sky

Stars look white at first glance, but they are actually many different colours. A star's colour depends on its average surface temperature and the energy of the light it emits. An iron bar heated in a furnace glows red at first but blue when it is hottest. The hottest stars also shine blue.

Blue star
Surface temperature: 30,000°C (54,000°F). The hottest stars shine with high-energy blue and ultraviolet lights.

White star
Surface temperature: 10,000°C (18,000°F). Hotter than our Sun, most white stars are also larger than the Sun, except for tiny, dim white dwarfs (see page 60).

Yellow star
Surface temperature: 5,500°C (9,900°F). The majority of yellow stars are similar in size to our Sun, but there are also huge yellow giants.

Orange star
Surface temperature: 4,000°C (7,200°F). Most cool orange stars are smaller than our Sun, except for huge orange giants near the ends of their lives.

Red star
Surface temperature: 3,000°C (5,400°F). Most red stars are small and insignificant. The brightest red stars in Earth's sky are all enormous but distant, dying stars – red giants.

Colourful wonders
The star clouds of the constellation Sagittarius (see pages 42–43) lie near the centre of the Milky Way. This superb Hubble Space Telescope image shows countless stars of different colours and brightness.

Size of a star

The size of a star is related to its colour and its brightness. Stars range in size from red dwarfs to blue giants, with our Sun lying somewhere in the middle of these two extremes. But when a star is dying, it increases in size and glows red, too.

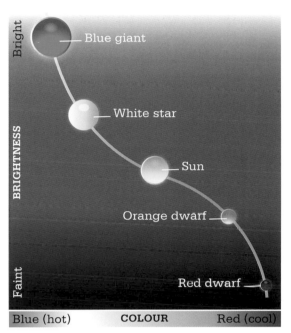

Main sequence
Most stars lie on what is known as the main sequence – the blue line shown here. Red stars are cool and faint, while blue stars are hot and bright. When stars are dying (see the red giant at right), they leave the sequence and become huge and bright.

Weight of a star

When astronomers find two stars orbiting a common point in space, they can work out the relative weights of each star. These weights reveal a pattern – dim red stars are small and light, while brilliant blue ones are larger and heavier.

Closer
The heavier star has a small orbit.

Farther
The lighter star has a wide orbit.

Seesaw effect
An adult sits closer to the centre of a seesaw to balance with a child.

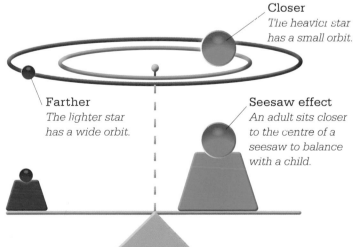

A balancing act
When an adult and a child sit on a seesaw, the heavier adult has to sit closer to the centre to keep it in balance. The same principle applies when two stars orbit a common point – the blue star orbiting nearer the middle must be heavier then the red star.

Life cycle of a star

By comparing the brightness, colours, sizes, and weights of stars, and adding what we know from studies of the Sun, astronomers can map out the life story of a typical star.

1 Star birth
Stars are born from collapsing gas clouds that grow large and dense enough to begin nuclear reactions (see page 40).

2 Star cluster
Although stars within a single cluster form around the same time, the rate at which they age depends on their weight (see page 42).

3 Main sequence
Stars spend most of their lives shining due to the nuclear fusion of hydrogen. During this period, the size of a star is related to its colour and brightness (see page 47).

4 Red giant
When a star runs out of hydrogen, it burns other elements, growing brighter and redder regardless of its weight (see page 53).

5 Death of a star

Planetary nebula
Light stars puff off their outer layers in shells (see page 56).

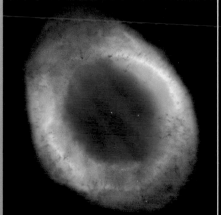

Supernova
The heaviest stars die in violent explosions (see page 58).

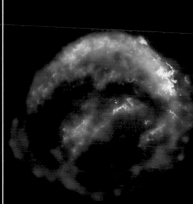

Orion [The Hunter]

One of the brightest and best-known constellations in the entire night sky is Orion. It is exceptional because parts of it can be seen from both the North and South Poles.

Constellation FACT FILE

Common name	The Hunter
Abbreviation	Ori
Visible from	Worldwide
Best time to see	December to March, after sunset
Brightest star	Rigel

Mid-latitude

LOCATION OF ORION

Origins

Ancient Greeks saw the pattern as the mighty hunter Orion. With his dogs Canis Major and Canis Minor, he faced the charging bull Taurus (see pages 58–59).

Orion confronts Taurus with a club.

Orion
This engraving shows how you can see the mythical figure of Orion in the stars.

"No other constellation more accurately represents the figure of a man"
–Germanicus Caesar (15 BCE–19 CE)

Orion's highlights

Many of Orion's interesting objects are quite close to one another. Its various nebulae, which are clouds of gas and dust, form parts of the huge Orion Molecular Cloud. Many of its bright stars were born from this cloud.

Orion's sword
A chain of bright young stars to the south of Orion's belt forms his sword.

Great Nebula
In the middle of the sword lies the Great Orion Nebula, a place where new stars are being born.

Betelgeuse
Pronounced "beetle juice", this brilliant red star marks Orion's shoulder. It is a red supergiant.

Rigel
This blue supergiant, about 775 light-years from Earth, is 70,000 times more luminous than our Sun.

Orion's belt
Look for three bright stars in a row (above). These form the belt across Orion's waist, making the constellation easy to spot.

Horsehead Nebula (NGC 2024)
This pillar of dust (left) looks like a horse's head silhouetted against more distant glowing gas.

Life of a star: Star birth

Stars are born in enormous clouds of gas and dust. Compressed by gravity, these clouds collapse under their own weight and separate into smaller knots of gas, which then grow dense enough to ignite as stars.

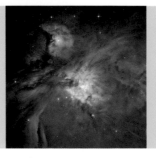

Great Orion Nebula
Fierce radiation from newborn stars at the heart of this nebula energizes the gas around it, causing it to glow.

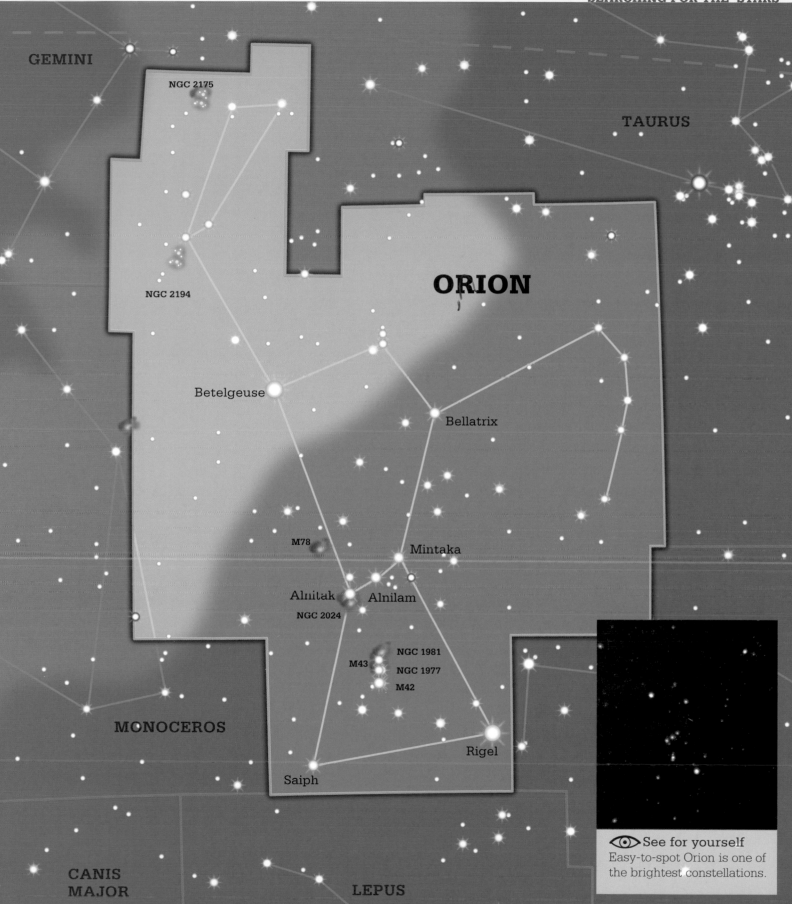

GEMINI

NGC 2175

TAURUS

NGC 2194

ORION

Betelgeuse

Bellatrix

M78

Mintaka

Alnitak   Alnilam

NGC 2024

NGC 1981

M43   NGC 1977

M42

MONOCEROS

Rigel

Saiph

CANIS
MAJOR

LEPUS

👁 See for yourself
Easy-to-spot Orion is one of
the brightest constellations.

Sagittarius [The Archer]

Rich in star clusters and nebulae (gas clouds), this vivid constellation lies in the southern half of the sky. It shines brightly because the middle of the Milky Way lies within its borders.

Constellation FACT FILE

Common name	The Archer
Abbreviation	Sgr
Visible from	Worldwide
Best time to see	July to October, after sunset
Brightest star	Kaus Australis

Southern Hemisphere

LOCATION OF SAGITTARIUS

Origins

For the ancient Greeks, Sagittarius represented a wise centaur named Chiron, an archer with a bow and arrow. A centaur has the torso of a man and the body of a horse.

Taking aim
Sagittarius points his arrow at the heart of the Scorpion (see pages 52–53).

Sagittarius' highlights

Sagittarius is home to star clouds, nebulae, and dust lanes that hide the centre of the Milky Way from view. It is famous for the teapot pattern formed by its eight central stars.

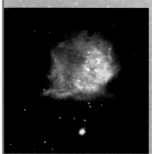

NGC 6822
This small, irregular galaxy, 1.8 million light-years from Earth, contains bright star-forming regions.

Omega/Swan Nebula (M17)
Dense clouds of gas pile up around the edges of this nebula.

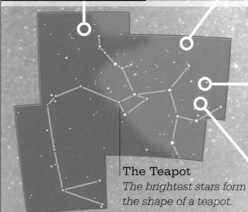

The Teapot
The brightest stars form the shape of a teapot.

Life of a star: Star clusters

Newborn stars emerge from nebulae in clusters. Those in an open cluster (an irregular group) drift apart over tens of millions of years – we see them only because there are so many short-lived, bright stars. Dense globular (globe-shaped) clusters hold together for much longer.

Globular cluster M22
This ball-shaped cluster in Sagittarius contains thousands of ageing stars.

Trifid Nebula (M20)
Dark dust lanes separate this famous star-forming nebula into three parts.

Lagoon Nebula (M8)
The Lagoon is one of the brightest nebulae. It is around 4,000 light-years from Earth.

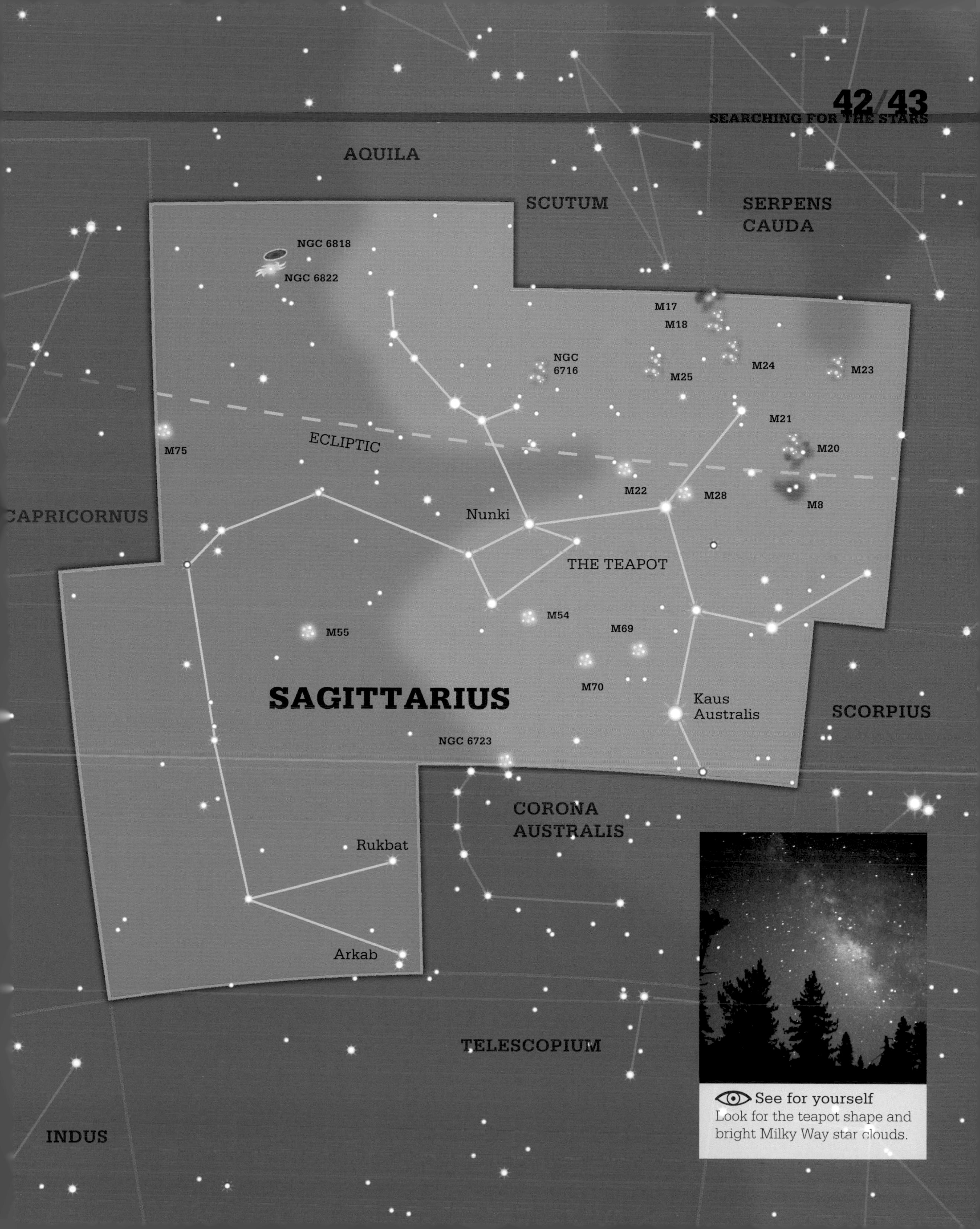

AQUILA

SCUTUM

SERPENS
CAUDA

NGC 6818

NGC 6822

M17

M18

NGC
6716

M25

M24

M23

M21

M20

M75

ECLIPTIC

M22

M28

M8

CAPRICORNUS

Nunki

THE TEAPOT

M54

M69

M55

SAGITTARIUS

M70

Kaus
Australis

SCORPIUS

NGC 6723

CORONA
AUSTRALIS

Rukbat

Arkab

TELESCOPIUM

INDUS

👁 **See for yourself**
Look for the teapot shape and
bright Milky Way star clouds.

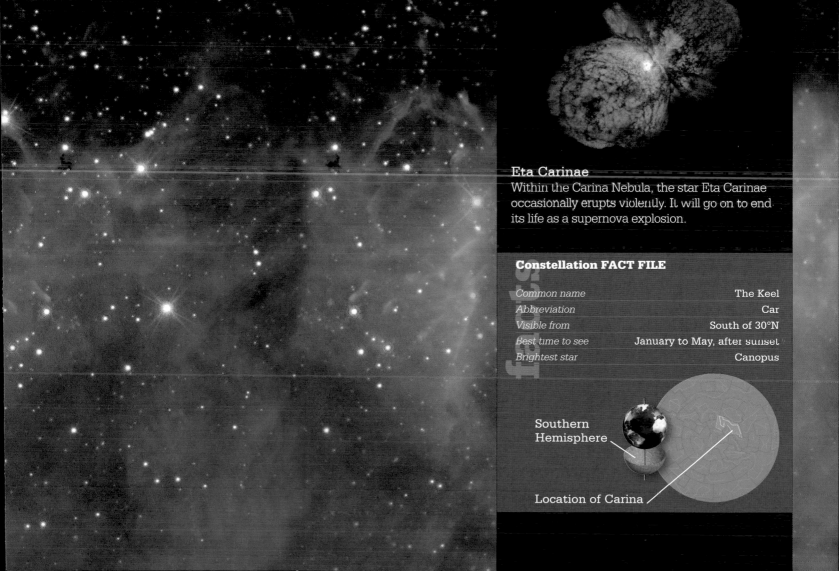

Eta Carinae

Within the Carina Nebula, the star Eta Carinae occasionally erupts violently. It will go on to end its life as a supernova explosion.

Constellation FACT FILE

Common name	The Keel
Abbreviation	Car
Visible from	South of 30°N
Best time to see	January to May, after sunset
Brightest star	Canopus

Southern Hemisphere

Location of Carina

Leo [The Lion]

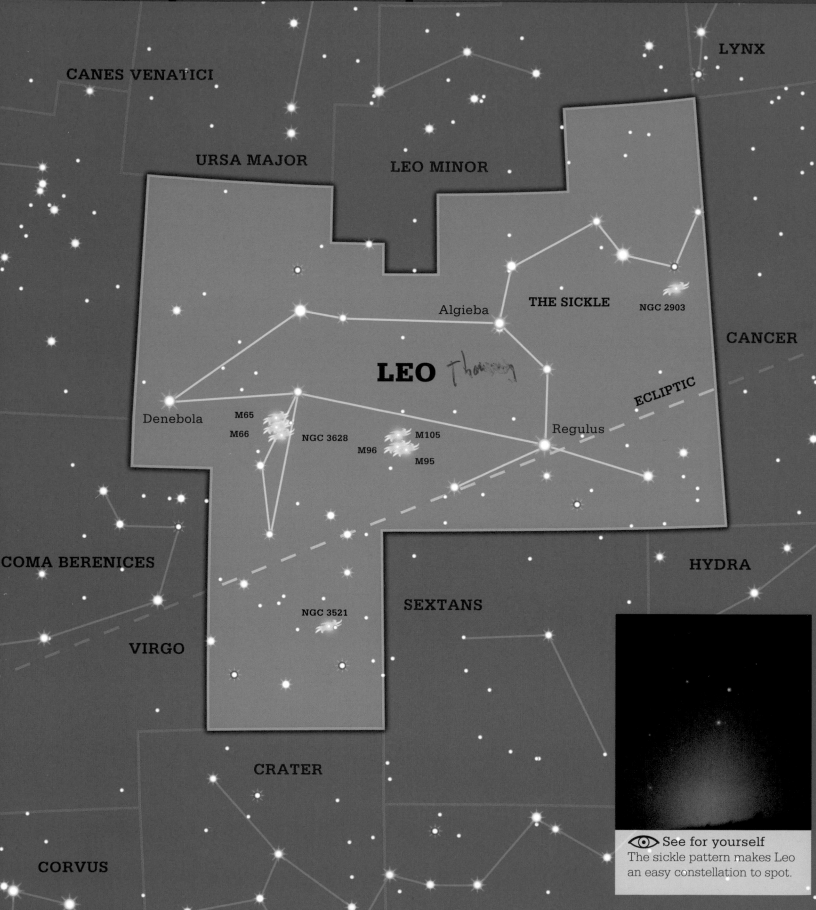

LYNX

CANES VENATICI

URSA MAJOR

LEO MINOR

THE SICKLE

NGC 2903

Algieba

CANCER

LEO

ECLIPTIC

Denebola

M65

M66

NGC 3628

M105

M96

M95

Regulus

COMA BERENICES

HYDRA

VIRGO

NGC 3521

SEXTANS

CRATER

CORVUS

👁 See for yourself
The sickle pattern makes Leo
an easy constellation to spot.

The constellation Leo, located in the Northern Hemisphere, resembles a crouching lion. Lying far from the band of the Milky Way, it is a good place to see distant galaxies.

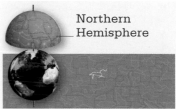

Constellation FACT FILE

Common name	The Lion
Abbreviation	Leo
Visible from	Worldwide
Best time to see	February to June, after sunset
Brightest star	Regulus

Northern Hemisphere

LOCATION OF LEO

Origins

Leo is usually said to represent the Nemean lion, a ferocious cave monster with an armoured hide. The Greek hero Heracles (Hercules to the Romans) had to fight this lion as one of 12 challenges.

Leo
For thousands of years, the constellation Leo has been viewed as a lion ready to pounce.

Wolf 359
in Leo is one of the closest stars
to Earth, but can be seen only **with a large telescope**

Leo's highlights

Most of Leo's brighter stars are in the main sequence of their lives (see box, right), so they show the link between a star's weight and its brightness. For example, the star Regulus is twice as far from Earth as Denebola, but it appears brighter because it is twice as heavy.

M96 galaxy
This spiral galaxy (above) lies at the heart of a small galaxy group, along with M95 and M105.

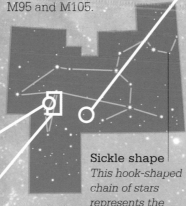

M66 galaxy
This spiral galaxy (above) has had its spiral arms distorted and its central nucleus pulled out of place by a close encounter with one of its neighbours.

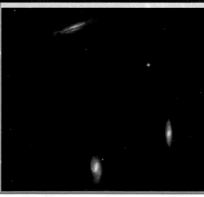

Sickle shape
This hook-shaped chain of stars represents the Lion's head.

Leo triplet
Three spiral galaxies, M65, M66, and NGC 3628 (left), form a small galaxy group near Leo's hind leg. This group is 35 million light-years from Earth.

Life of a star: Main sequence

After an unstable youth, a star spends most of its life shining through hydrogen fusion. In this stage, called the main sequence, the star's brightness depends on its weight (see page 39). The heavier a star is, the hotter and denser its core, and the brighter it shines. Bright stars use their fuel more rapidly and die sooner.

Regulus
The brightest star in Leo is Regulus, 78 light-years from Earth. Lying close to the ecliptic, it is regularly hidden from view from the Earth by the Moon.

The Universe is absolutely enormous, and the spaces between planets, stars, and galaxies are so big that it is impossible for us to visualize them in everyday units of measurement. This is why astronomers use much bigger units of measurement.

177 years: the length of time it would take to drive to the Sun at 100 kph (60 mph)

The solar system . . . and beyond

Measurements such as kilometres and miles become useless beyond Earth. The distances in interplanetary space are so huge that a good way for us to comprehend them is to reduce space objects to sizes we can understand.

If this dot represents the size of Earth, then . . .

Moon

. . . the Moon would be 1.5 cm (0.5 in) away, and . . .

Relative distances
By reducing the Earth to the size of a dot and its orbit of the Sun to a small circle, we can better understand its proximity to other space objects.

Sun

. . . the Sun would be a ball 55 cm (21.5 in) across and 6 m (19.7 ft) away.

If this circle represents the orbit of Earth around the Sun, then . . .

Neptune

. . . Neptune's average orbit would be a circle 15 cm (6 in) across, and . . .

Proxima Centauri

. . . Proxima Centauri, the nearest star to the Sun, would be 0.6 km (0.4 miles) away.

Space travel
A spacecraft travelling at 100,000 kph (60,000 mph) would still take 46,000 *years* to reach Proxima Centauri, the closest star to the Sun!

Not so fast!
Science-fiction spacecraft travel much faster than their real-life counterparts.

At the speed of light

One way to make sense of the scale of the Universe is to look at how much time light takes to cross huge cosmic distances. Light, the fastest thing in the Universe, moves at 300,000 km (186,000 miles) per second.

Light leaving the Sun takes . . .

8 minutes, 20 seconds . . . to reach Earth.

2 hours . . . to reach Neptune.

1 year . . . to reach the outer edge of the Oort Cloud, the farthest extent of our solar system.

4.2 years . . . to reach Proxima Centauri, the closest star to the Sun.

Light-years
One light-year is the distance that light travels in a year. It is equivalent to 9.5 million million km (5.9 million million miles).

Looking back in time

We see space objects as they were when light left them, so when we look into the Universe, we look back in time. The farther we look, the further back in cosmic time we see. Some galaxies may be so far away, their light hasn't reached Earth yet – perhaps it never will.

Early humans
We see the Andromeda galaxy as it was when the first humans were living, 2.5 million years ago.

Roman times
At 2,000 light-years away, the M25 star cluster in Sagittarius appears to us now as it was during the Roman Empire.

Stonehenge
Light from the Eagle Nebula (M16) began its journey to Earth 5,500 years ago, when Stonehenge was being built in ancient Britain.

Dinosaurs
Light left galaxy NGC 406, in the southern constellation Tucana, 65 million years ago, in the age of the dinosaurs.

Cygnus [The Swan]

Also known as the Northern Cross, Cygnus makes a distinctive pattern against the rich star clouds of the northern Milky Way. It has many fascinating stars and nebulae.

Constellation FACT FILE

Common name	The Swan
Abbreviation	Cyg
Visible from	Worldwide
Best time to see	July to November, after sunset
Brightest star	Deneb

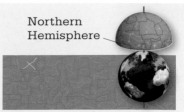
Northern Hemisphere
LOCATION OF CYGNUS

Origins

In Greek myth, Cygnus was the god Zeus in disguise. He changed into a swan to visit a beautiful woman named Leda.

Swan's tail
The star Deneb represents the tail of Cygnus.

Swan's beak
The binary star Albireo marks the tip of the Swan's beak.

Cygnus and Phaeton
In another myth about Cygnus, he was a god transformed into a swan by Zeus to retrieve the body of his friend Phaeton from a river.

Cygnus' highlights

The position of Cygnus against a dense region of the Milky Way makes it a great place to look for unusual objects. These include a famous binary star, a likely black hole (see pages 60–61), and one of the most luminous stars in the sky, Deneb.

Deneb
Cygnus' brightest star is 2,500 light-years from Earth. It is about 160,000 times brighter than the Sun.

Cygnus Rift
A "gap" in the Milky Way shows where dark dust is blocking the light of more distant stars.

North America Nebula (NGC 7000)
Resembling the shape of North America, this nebula is just visible to the naked eye.

Cygnus X-1
This is a superdense black hole that pulls in nearby matter and gives off X-rays.

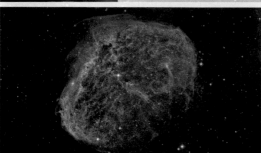

Crescent Nebula (NGC 6888)
This glowing bubble (above) was created by gas blowing out from a central star at high speeds.

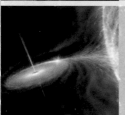

Veil Nebula (NGC 6992)
The brightest part of the Cygnus Loop, the Veil Nebula is a 60,000-year-old remnant of a supernova (see page 58).

Life of a star: Binaries

Some of the larger knots of gas within star-forming nebulae collapse to form two or more stars. These double (known as binary) or multiple stars usually end up locked in orbit around one another for the rest of their lives.

Albireo
At the southern end of Cygnus, Albireo's yellow and blue components make it one of the most beautiful binaries.

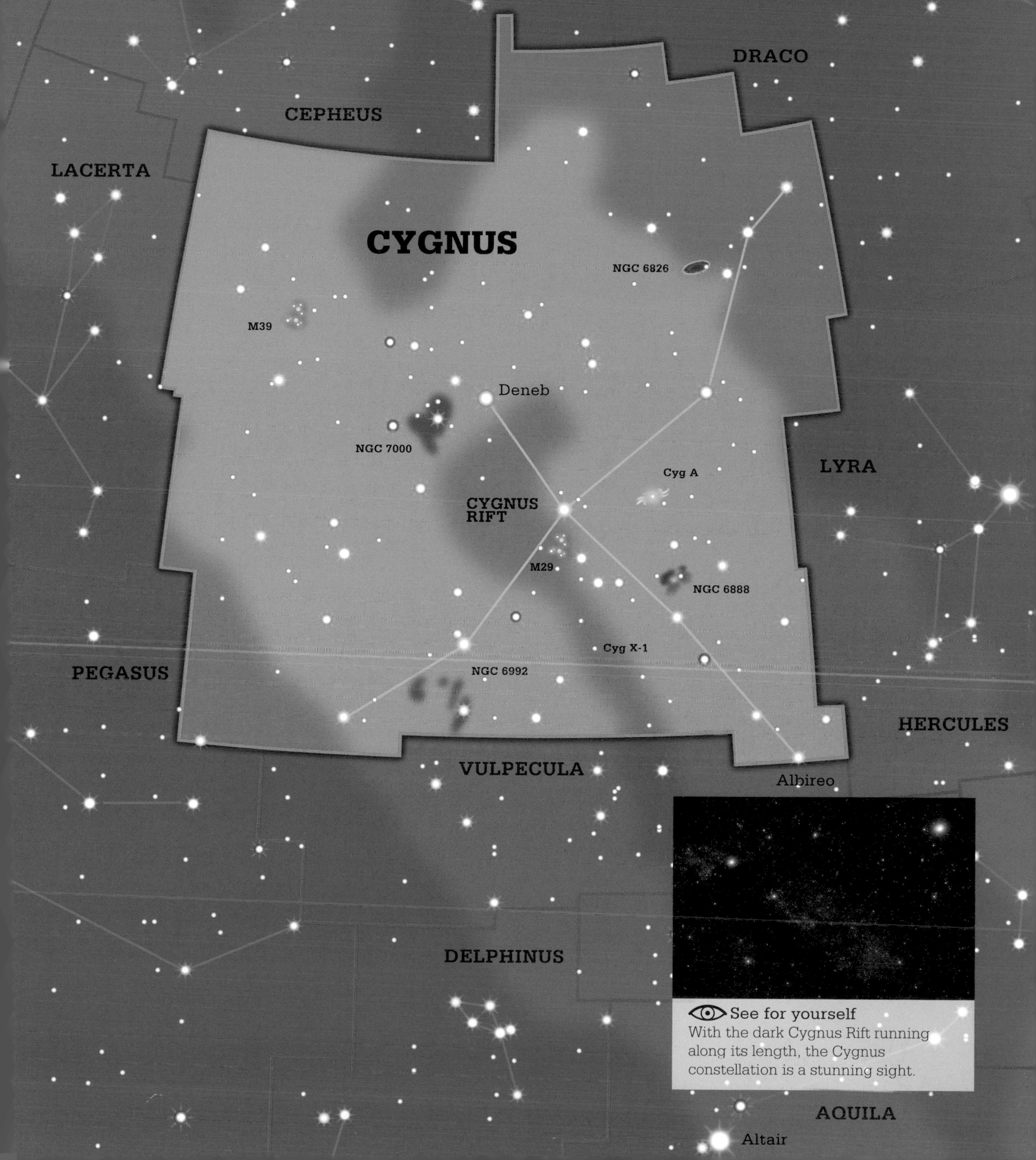

DRACO

CEPHEUS

LACERTA

CYGNUS

NGC 6826

M39

Deneb

NGC 7000

LYRA

Cyg A

**CYGNUS
RIFT**

M29

NGC 6888

Cyg X-1

PEGASUS

NGC 6992

HERCULES

VULPECULA

Albireo

👁 See for yourself
With the dark Cygnus Rift running
along its length, the Cygnus
constellation is a stunning sight.

DELPHINUS

AQUILA

Altair

Scorpius [The Scorpion]

SERPENS
CAUDA

OPHIUCHUS

SAGITTARIUS

ECLIPTIC

M80

Antares

M4

LIBRA

SCORPIUS

LUPUS

M6

NGC
6383

NGC 6357/
Pismis 24

M7

NGC
6334

Shaula

NGC
6124

NGC 6322

NGC
6231

CORONA
AUSTRALIS

NGC 6388

NGC
6178

NORMA

ARA

See for yourself
Find Scorpius by looking for
Antares and its flanking stars.

Scorpius lies at the southern end of the zodiac, close to the centre of the Milky Way. This constellation contains some spectacular stars, nebulae, and star clusters.

Constellation FACT FILE

Common name	The Scorpion
Abbreviation	Sco
Visible from	Worldwide
Best time to see	April to September, after sunset
Brightest star	Antares

Southern Hemisphere

LOCATION OF SCORPIUS

Origins

In Greek mythology, the hunter Orion (see pages 40 41) was killed by a scorpion's sting. Other myths claim that a scorpion scared Phaeton's flying horses, causing his death (see page 50).

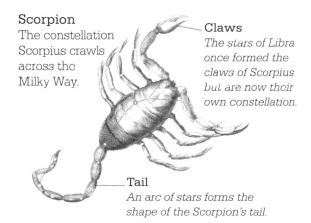

Scorpion
The constellation Scorpius crawls across the Milky Way.

Claws
The stars of Libra once formed the claws of Scorpius but are now their own constellation.

Tail
An arc of stars forms the shape of the Scorpion's tail.

Life of a star: Red giants

When a star runs out of fuel in its core at the end of its life, it keeps on shining by burning hydrogen in shells around the core. This causes it to brighten and swell in size, so its surface cools and it turns orange or red. Depending on its size, it is then called a giant or a supergiant.

Supergiant
Embedded in a glowing cloud of gas, Antares is 65,000 times brighter than the Sun.

Scorpius' highlights

Many of the bright stars in Scorpius are true neighbours in space. They were formed around the same time from the same cloud of star-forming material.

Betelgeuse

Antares

Our Sun

Antares
Antares has a radius of 1 billion kilometres (600 million miles).

M4 star cluster
A globular cluster (see page 42) lies to the west of Antares.

Stinger
The multiple star Shaula marks the Scorpion's tail.

Pismis 24 and NGC 6357
This star cluster and associated nebulae contain one of the most massive and luminous stars known.

Cat's Paw Nebula (NGC 6334)
These distinctive blotches are clouds of glowing gas, energized from within by newborn stars that are more than ten times the mass of the Sun.

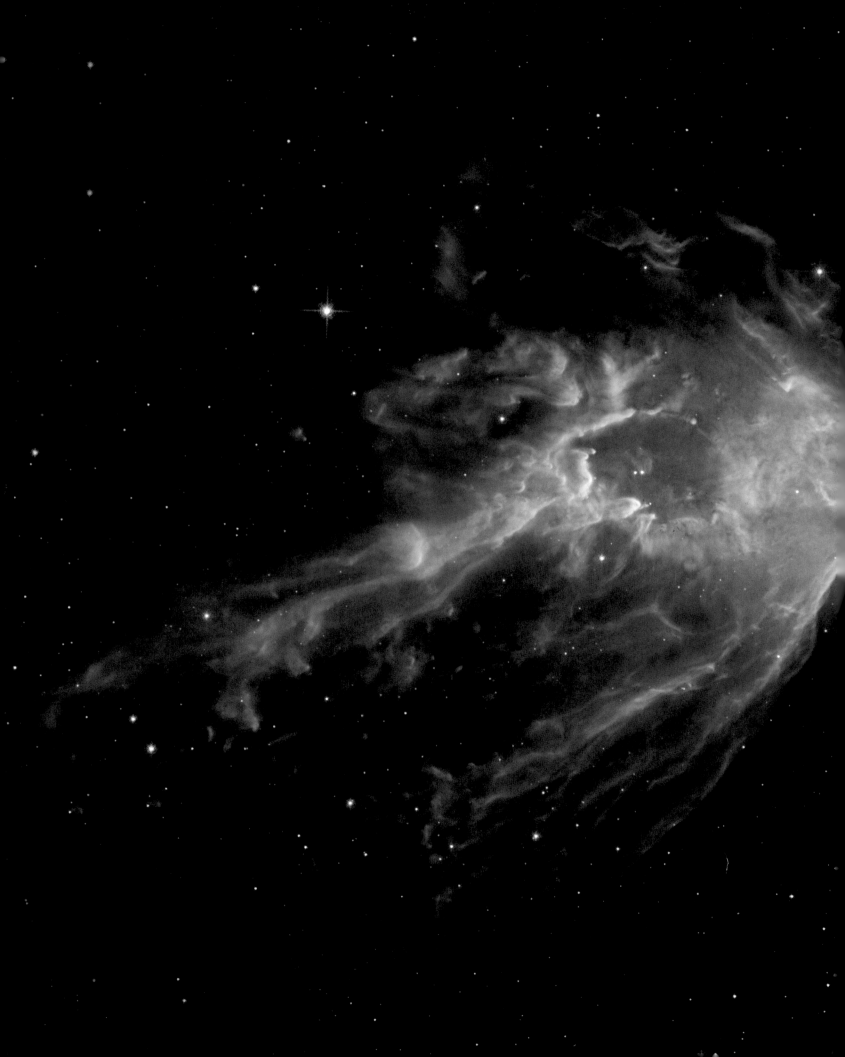

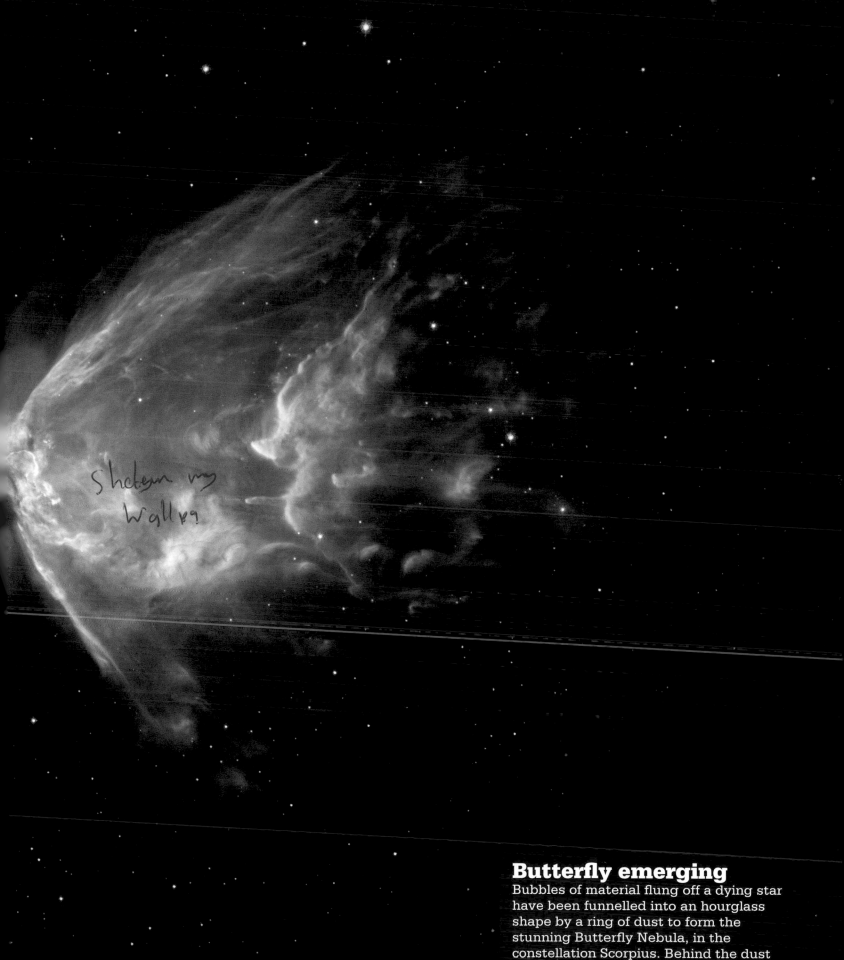

Butterfly emerging

Bubbles of material flung off a dying star have been funnelled into an hourglass shape by a ring of dust to form the stunning Butterfly Nebula, in the constellation Scorpius. Behind the dust lies one of the galaxy's hottest stars, burning at 200,000°C (360,000°F).

Lyra [The Lyre]

An ancient musical instrument, the lyre, gives its name to this small constellation in the northern skies. Despite its size, Lyra is packed with magnificent stars and other objects.

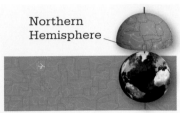

Northern Hemisphere

LOCATION OF LYRA

Origins

In Greek mythology, the lyre – a harp-like instrument – was played by the doomed musician Orpheus (far right).

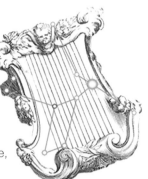

Making music
It was said that when Orpheus played the lyre, it tamed wild animals.

Lost love
Orpheus used music to win back his dead wife, Eurydice, from the Underworld, where the souls of the dead dwelled. But he forgot his promise not to look at her until they were back on Earth, and he lost her again forever.

Lyra's highlights

On the edge of the northern Milky Way, Lyra contains several incredible stars showing different stages in a stellar life cycle.

Bright neighbour
At a distance of just 25 light-years from Earth, Vega is the fifth-brightest star in our skies.

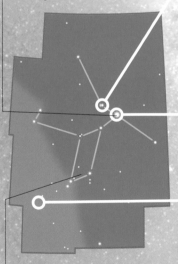

Ring Nebula
This famous planetary nebula lies midway between Lyra's two southernmost stars and can be seen with a small telescope.

Epsilon Lyrae
This amazing quadruple star contains two double stars orbiting each other.

Vega
A bright young star (above), Vega is surrounded by a disk of dusty material that may be forming a new planetary system.

Cluster M56
This star cluster is about 33,000 light-years from Earth.

Life of a star: Dying stars

Eventually, all stars run out of fuel and can no longer keep shining. If a star has roughly the mass of the Sun, it will become an unstable red giant, pulsating and finally flinging off its outer layers in a glowing shell called a planetary nebula. The hot, exhausted core left behind shrinks into a dense white dwarf star (see page 60).

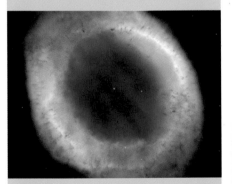

Ring Nebula (M57)
This planetary nebula in Lyra, the remnant of a dying star, forms a ring of gas. Planetary nebulae can look like planets at first glance.

SAGITTA

R Lyrae

LYRA

RR Lyrae

CYGNUS

Epsilon Lyrae

Vega

HERCULES

M57

M56

VULPECULA

👁 See for yourself
Lyra is easily spotted, thanks
to its bright star Vega.

SAGITTA

Taurus [The Bull]

Instantly recognizable, Taurus (Latin for "bull") looks like the front of a mighty bull charging through the sky towards Orion. It's also home to several intriguing deep-sky objects.

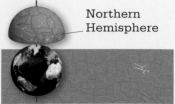

Northern Hemisphere

LOCATION OF TAURUS

Origins

Taurus is such an obvious bull-like star pattern that it has been recognized since the most ancient times. It may even be depicted in prehistoric cave paintings.

Bull's horn
The star that marks Taurus' upper horn is shared with the neighbouring constellation Auriga.

Taurus, the Bull
The distinctive constellation looks like the head and raised front legs of a bull.

Life of a star: Supernovae

As a really massive star grows older, it keeps shining by burning heavier elements. Eventually, though, it collapses under its own weight, triggering a brilliant supernova explosion.

Crab Nebula
These shreds of superhot gas are the expanding remains of a supernova explosion in Taurus, which was seen on Earth in 1054.

Taurus' highlights

Home to two of the most obvious star clusters in Earth's skies, Taurus also contains a supernova remnant from an explosion thousands of years ago.

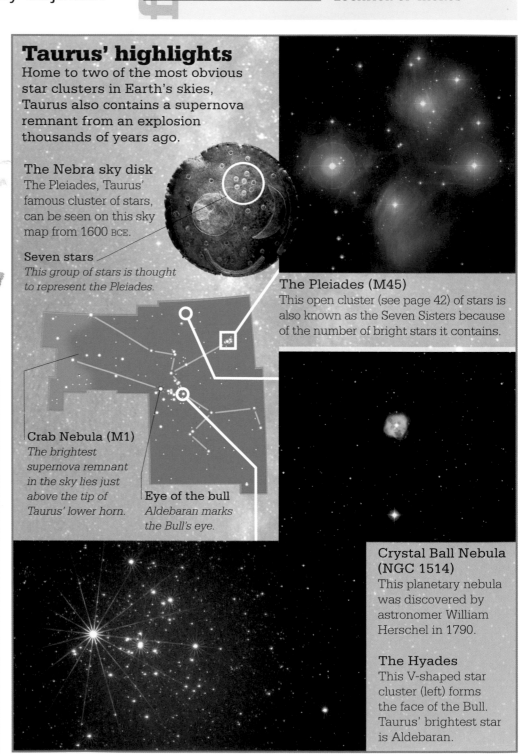

The Nebra sky disk
The Pleiades, Taurus' famous cluster of stars, can be seen on this sky map from 1600 BCE.

Seven stars
This group of stars is thought to represent the Pleiades.

Crab Nebula (M1)
The brightest supernova remnant in the sky lies just above the tip of Taurus' lower horn.

Eye of the bull
Aldebaran marks the Bull's eye.

The Pleiades (M45)
This open cluster (see page 42) of stars is also known as the Seven Sisters because of the number of bright stars it contains.

Crystal Ball Nebula (NGC 1514)
This planetary nebula was discovered by astronomer William Herschel in 1790.

The Hyades
This V-shaped star cluster (left) forms the face of the Bull. Taurus' brightest star is Aldebaran.

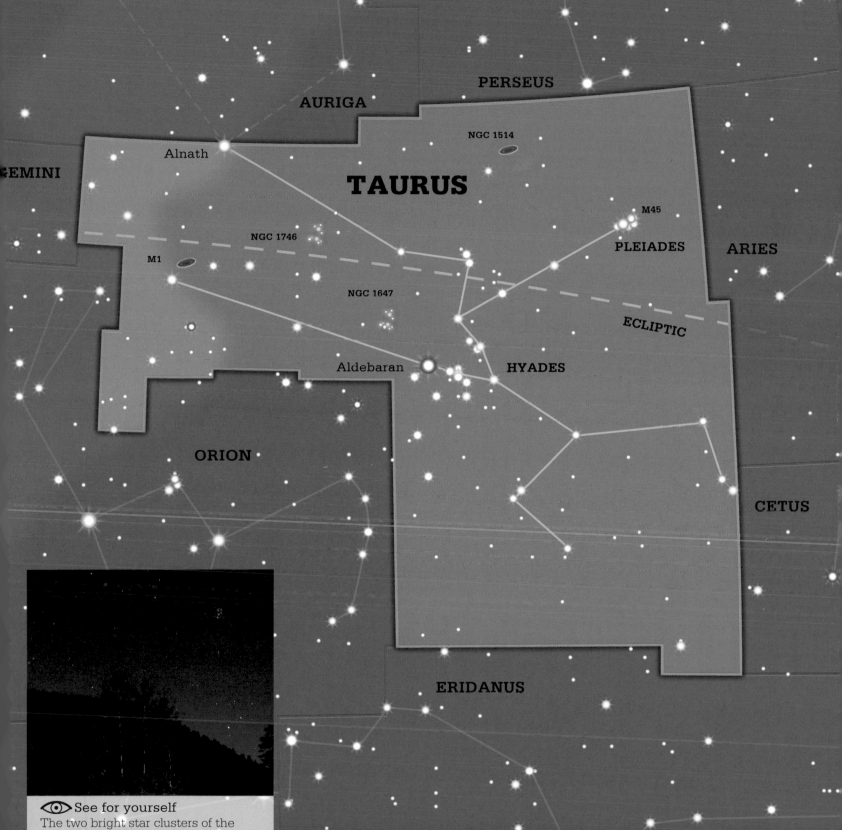

PERSEUS

AURIGA

NGC 1514

Alnath

GEMINI

TAURUS

M45

NGC 1746

PLEIADES

ARIES

M1

NGC 1647

ECLIPTIC

Aldebaran

HYADES

ORION

CETUS

ERIDANUS

👁 See for yourself
The two bright star clusters of the Hyades and Pleiades make Taurus an easy constellation to spot

When a star dies, its remnant, in the form of a superdense burned-out core, collapses. These dead stars can then go on to form some of the strangest objects in the Universe.

Black holes

Very rarely, the weight of a dying star's core is so great that it collapses until all its matter is jammed into a single point. This point seals itself off from the Universe behind a wall called the event horizon. Nothing can escape it.

Spaghettification

If you fell into a black hole, it would pull on your feet more than on your head, stretching you out like spaghetti!

X-rays
Matter falling into the black hole is heated up until it emits high-energy X-rays.

Matter
Objects that get too close to the hole are sucked in.

Warped space
Objects and light passing the hole are deflected from their original courses.

White dwarfs

Once a star like the Sun has blown off its outer layers in a planetary nebula (see page 56), all that is left is the core. This becomes a faint but hot white dwarf, roughly the size of Earth.

Diamond core
A white dwarf is rich in carbon, the same element that, when compressed, forms diamonds.

The hottest known white dwarf has a temperature of 200,000°C (360,000°F)

Neutron stars

Stars that weigh as much as eight Suns die in supernova explosions. The forces involved split the stars' atoms and jam the surviving neutron particles together in fast-spinning, very dense neutron stars.

A pinhead's worth of neutron star weighs the same as a supertanker

Event horizon
Nothing, not even light, can escape beyond this point.

Gravity well

Heavyweight star
A neutron star is the densest physical object in the Universe.

The first black hole to be identified was Cygnus X-1, 6,000 light-years away from Earth

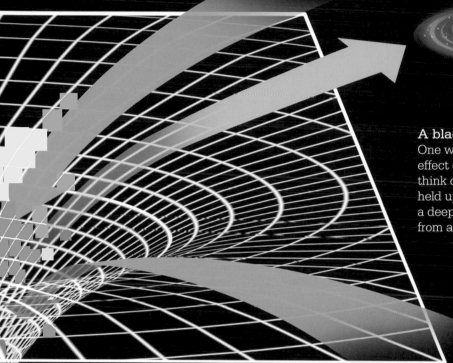

A black hole in space
One way to imagine the effect of a black hole is to think of space as a flat sheet held up and pulled tight, with a deep dent in the middle from a superdense object.

More here

A Black Hole Is Not a Hole by Carolyn Cinami DeCristofano

Scientists in the Field: The Mysterious Universe by Nic Bishop and Ellen Jackson

black hole
event horizon **pulsar**
spaghettification
Cygnus X-1
white dwarf
neutron star

See for yourself – there's a white dwarf orbiting the brightest star in the sky, Sirius. But the easiest one to see with binoculars is called Eridanus, in the southern hemisphere.

planetary nebula: the gas shell thrown off when a red star dies.

supernova: the blast created when a massive star explodes at the end of its normal life.

X-ray: a form of radiation produced by stars and hot gas clouds.

Pulsars

A neutron star (see opposite page) compresses most of a star's original magnetism into a tiny space. This creates a powerful field that channels radiation from the star along two narrow beams. Often, the result is a rapidly flashing pulsar.

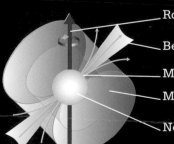

Rotation axis

Beam of radio waves

Magnetic pole

Magnetic field

Neutron star

Pulsing pulsars
A pulsar is a bit like a cosmic lighthouse. It may flash hundreds of times per second as the star rotates rapidly.

Pulsar flashes
A pulsar only appears "on" when its beam points straight at Earth.

PULSAR OFF **PULSAR ON** **PULSAR OFF**

Discoverin
plar

* Why did people believe there was life on Mars?

* Who took "one small step"?

* What creates a planet's incredible rings?

g amazing

nets

The planets are spherical objects that orbit the Sun. They are often accompanied by moons, which orbit them in turn (see pages 86–87). There are eight planets: four smaller rocky planets in the inner solar system, and four larger gas giants farther from the Sun.

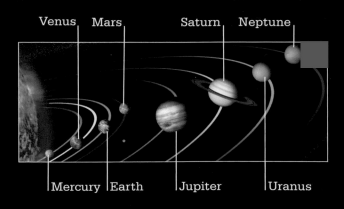

Venus   Mars   Saturn   Neptune

Mercury Earth   Jupiter   Uranus

Rocky planets

Mercury, Venus, Earth, and Mars are all rocky planets. Dominated by solid rock, their surfaces are hard enough to stand on. The rocks inside these planets have separated into layers depending on their weights, producing a core of solid or molten iron and a surface of relatively light rock.

The Sun weighs
743x
more than all the planets put together

Mercury
The smallest of the major planets, Mercury is only slightly larger than Earth's Moon.

Earth
Our home is the largest of the rocky planets. Its molten core powers volcanoes, and it has a dense atmosphere. It is the only planet with oceans.

Venus
The second-largest rocky planet, Venus is just a little smaller than Earth. It is very different from Earth, however, with a dense, toxic atmosphere and searing temperatures.

Sun
The Sun lies at the centre of our solar system and dwarfs the planets. Its powerful gravity keeps them in orbit around it.

Mars
The outermost rocky planet, Mars is about half the size of Earth, with a thin atmosphere and a cold, dry surface.

View from Earth
These images show the other seven planets as seen through a large, high-quality backyard telescope.

MERCURY   VENUS   MARS

Gas giants

Jupiter, Saturn, Uranus, and Neptune are huge compared to the rocky planets. They are mostly deep layers of gas with only small solid cores at their centres.

Jupiter

The biggest planet of all, Jupiter spins so rapidly that it bulges outwards at its equator, making it noticeably oval.

Uranus

This is a gigantic ball of gas and liquid. This strange world was the first to be discovered with a telescope.

Saturn

This was the most distant planet known to ancient astronomers, but its famous rings were not discovered until the telescope was invented (see page 18).

Neptune

The most distant major planet, Neptune is a ball of cold, slushy ice. Its outer atmosphere has the fiercest winds in the solar system.

See for yourself

Distant giants look much smaller than nearby planets because they are so far away.

JUPITER

SATURN

URANUS

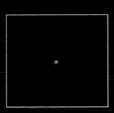
NEPTUNE

More here

War of the Worlds
by H. G. Wells

Who Is Neil Armstrong?
by Roberta Edwards

KidsAstronomy.com
NASA **gas giants**
rocky planets methane
solar system

Join the NASA Kids' Club
at www.nasa.gov/
audience/forkids/kidsclub/
flash/index.html.

*A Traveller's Guide to
the Planets* (National
Geographic, 2010)

Visit the Peter Harrison Planetarium at the Royal Observatory, Greenwich, London, for amazing shows that use real images from spacecraft and telescopes. Fly to distant galaxies, watch the birth of a star, and land on Mars.

Go to the National Space Centre, Leicester for the UK's largest planetarium.

Driving on the Moon

Six Apollo missions landed on the Moon from 1969 to 1972 (see page 71). On the final three missions, a "Moon buggy" (the Lunar Roving Vehicle, or LRV) enabled further exploration of the Moon's surface. Here, James Irwin of Apollo 15 and the LRV are near the foot of Mount Hadley.

Mercury and Venus [Rocky]

Two planets – Mercury and Venus – orbit nearer to the Sun than Earth does (see page 66). For this reason, they are never seen far from the Sun. Mercury is a tiny, fast-moving planet with a scorched, airless surface. Venus is a near twin of Earth in size, cloaked in a dense atmosphere.

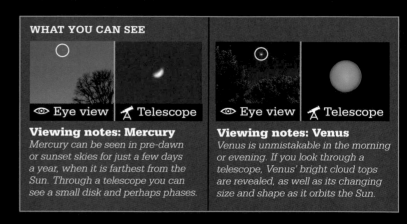

WHAT YOU CAN SEE

👁 Eye view | 🔭 Telescope

👁 Eye view | 🔭 Telescope

Viewing notes: Mercury
Mercury can be seen in pre-dawn or sunset skies for just a few days a year, when it is farthest from the Sun. Through a telescope you can see a small disk and perhaps phases.

Viewing notes: Venus
Venus is unmistakable in the morning or evening. If you look through a telescope, Venus' bright cloud tops are revealed, as well as its changing size and shape as it orbits the Sun.

Mercury

It takes less than three months for Mercury to orbit the Sun. It is only visible just before dawn or just after sunset and looks very much like Earth's Moon, with a heavily cratered surface and no air. But it is much hotter – the temperature on Mercury can get hot enough to melt lead. One of Mercury's strangest features is its enormous metal core, which makes up about 40 per cent of its interior.

Mercury

Diameter	4,880 km (3,032 miles) – 0.38 x Earth
Mass (compared to Earth)	0.06 x Earth
Gravity (compared to Earth)	0.38 x Earth
Rotation period (day)	59 days
Number of moons	0

The surface of Mercury reaches 427°C (801°F)

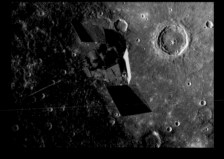

MESSENGER to Mercury
Mercury moves so fast that it is very difficult to reach with spacecraft. *MESSENGER*, the first probe to study Mercury in detail, took seven years to enter its orbit, finally arriving in 2011.

Water on Mercury?
While temperatures soar in daylight, Mercury is a freezing –180°C (–290°F) at night. Deep impact craters near Mercury's poles never get sunlight at all. Astronomers think they might be filled with ice left behind by collisions with comets.

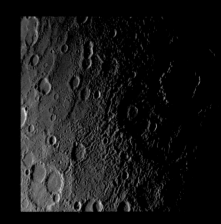

Cratered world
Mercury is dimpled by countless craters from ancient impacts.

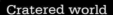

Venus

The closest planet to Earth, Venus shines brilliantly in the morning or evening sky. As Venus orbits the Sun, we see different amounts of its sunlit side, giving Venus phases just like those of Earth's Moon (see pages 68–69). The phases can be seen through a small telescope.

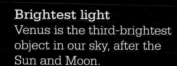

Brightest light

Venus is the third-brightest object in our sky, after the Sun and Moon.

Venus

Diameter	12,102 km (7,520 miles) – 0.95 x Earth
Mass (compared to Earth)	0.82 x Earth
Gravity (compared to Earth)	0.91 x Earth
Rotation period (day)	243 days
Number of moons	0

Choking atmosphere

Venus' atmosphere is far denser than Earth's, and dominated by toxic carbon dioxide. It heats the planet to around 460°C (860°F) and exerts crushing pressures.

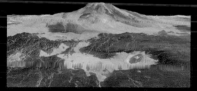

Beneath the clouds

Space probes can fire radar beams into Venus' atmosphere to map its surface.

Landing on Venus

From the 1960s to 1980s, a series of Russian *Venera* space probes tried to land on Venus. The first melted before they reached the surface, but with heavy shielding later missions, such as Venera 14, sent back pictures for a few minutes.

Volcanic world

Radar maps of Venus reveal a planet shaped by volcanic eruptions.

Mars [The red one]

Famous for its red colour, Mars is one of the most visible planets. Despite having a cold, dry surface, it is the most Earth-like of the rocky planets, with huge amounts of hidden water.

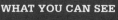
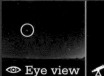
Surface of Mars

Mars' landscape is a mixture of heavily cratered highlands and lowland plains. It is covered in evidence of past natural activity, from huge volcanoes to floodplains and river valleys. Mars' poles even have bright ice caps similar to those on Earth.

Mars rovers
NASA has sent wheeled robots to Mars to investigate this fascinating planet.

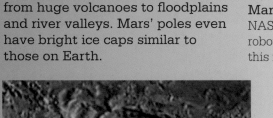

Icy planet
Ice caps on Mars are made of frozen carbon dioxide or "dry ice" above buried water ice.

River valley
Mars has steep-sided valleys carved by flowing water. This is evidence that the planet was once warmer and wetter than it is today.

Mars looks red-hot but is in **fact very** cold

Olympus Mons

Tharsis volcano chain

Mars

Diameter	6,795 km (4,222 miles) – 0.53 x Earth
Mass (compared to Earth)	0.107 x Earth
Gravity (compared to Earth)	0.38 x Earth
Rotation period (day)	24 hours, 39 minutes
Number of moons	2

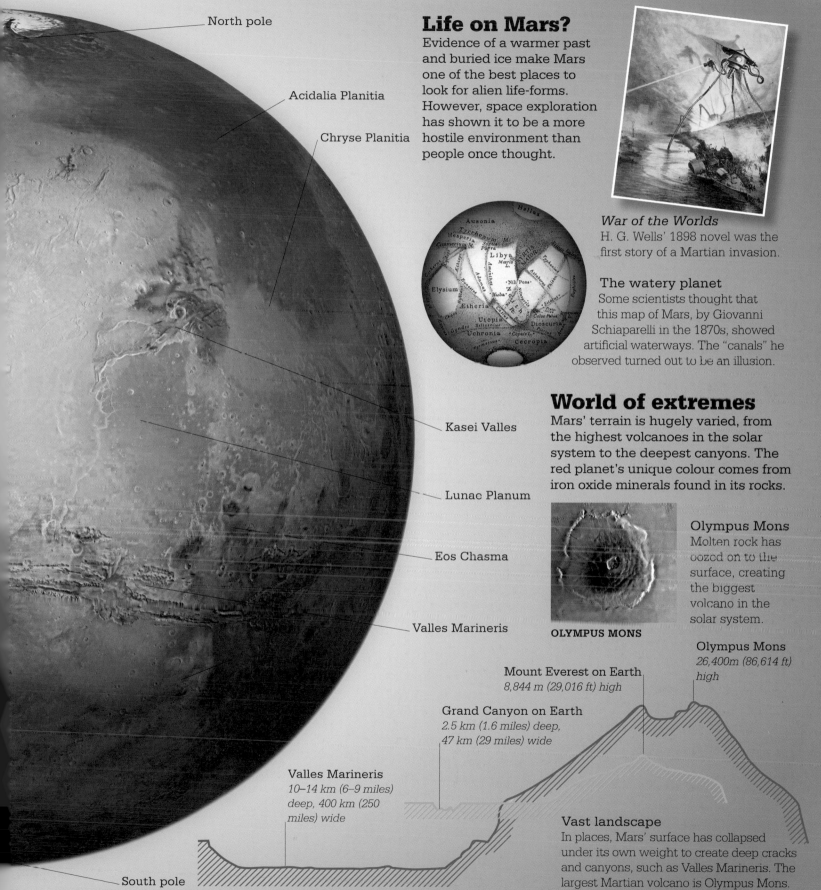

North pole

Acidalia Planitia

Chryse Planitia

Kasei Valles

Lunac Planum

Eos Chasma

Valles Marineris

South pole

Life on Mars?

Evidence of a warmer past and buried ice make Mars one of the best places to look for alien life-forms. However, space exploration has shown it to be a more hostile environment than people once thought.

War of the Worlds
H. G. Wells' 1898 novel was the first story of a Martian invasion.

The watery planet
Some scientists thought that this map of Mars, by Giovanni Schiaparelli in the 1870s, showed artificial waterways. The "canals" he observed turned out to be an illusion.

World of extremes

Mars' terrain is hugely varied, from the highest volcanoes in the solar system to the deepest canyons. The red planet's unique colour comes from iron oxide minerals found in its rocks.

Olympus Mons
Molten rock has oozed on to the surface, creating the biggest volcano in the solar system.

OLYMPUS MONS

Olympus Mons
26,400m (86,614 ft) high

Mount Everest on Earth
8,844 m (29,016 ft) high

Grand Canyon on Earth
2.5 km (1.6 miles) deep, 47 km (29 miles) wide

Valles Marineris
10–14 km (6–9 miles) deep, 400 km (250 miles) wide

Vast landscape
In places, Mars' surface has collapsed under its own weight to create deep cracks and canyons, such as Valles Marineris. The largest Martian volcano is Olympus Mons.

Jupiter [The giant]

The biggest planet in the solar system, Jupiter could contain all the others with room to spare. It is a giant ball of gas surrounded by bands of light and dark clouds, with fierce storms that can grow larger than the entire Earth.

Jupiter

Diameter	142,984 km (88,846 miles) – 11.21 x Earth
Mass (compared to Earth)	318 x Earth
Gravity (compared to Earth)	2.53 x Earth
Rotation period (day)	9 hours, 56 minutes
Number of moons	63

Red spots

Jupiter's most obvious feature is a red oval known as the Great Red Spot (GRS), which is an atmospheric storm twice the size of Earth. The GRS has been visible to astronomers for at least 200 years; it is sometimes accompanied by other, smaller spots.

Getting up close
This colour picture of Jupiter was taken by the *Cassini* space probe in 2000.

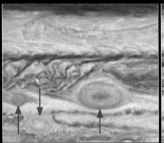 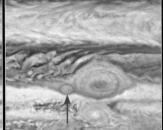 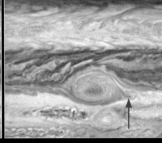

15 May, 2008
Three red spots circle Jupiter in its southern hemisphere.

28 June, 2008
The smallest spot begins to collide with the Great Red Spot.

8 July, 2008
The smallest spot is absorbed completely by the giant storm.

Gas giant

Jupiter's gaseous content makes it more like the Sun than any other planet. It will never be possible to land on Jupiter. The bands, swirls, and spots on its surface are all a result of its cloudy atmosphere.

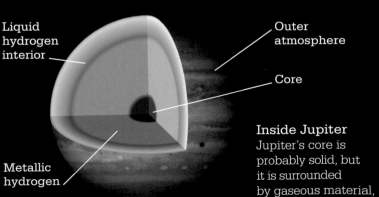

Liquid hydrogen interior

Outer atmosphere

Core

Metallic hydrogen

Inside Jupiter
Jupiter's core is probably solid, but it is surrounded by gaseous material, mainly hydrogen.

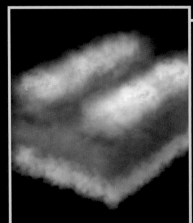

Jupiter's surface
It is the bright yellow and red clouds swirling around Jupiter that give it such a striking, colourful appearance.

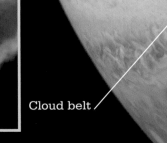

Cloud belt

Great Red Spot

CALLISTO

GANYMEDE

EUROPA

IO

Jupiter's moons

Jupiter has a huge family of 63 known moons, 4 of which are roughly the size of Earth's Moon. These 4 moons (at left) were discovered by Italian astronomer Galileo in 1609. They are known as the Galilean moons.

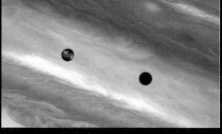

Io casts a shadow

When moons pass in front of Jupiter, they cast shadows on its surface. When they pass behind Jupiter, the planet eclipses – or obscures – them.

Comet catcher

Jupiter's vast size and gravity cause comets and asteroids to crash-land into it. These huge explosions leave long-lasting dark "scars" in Jupiter's clouds.

59 more

63 moons

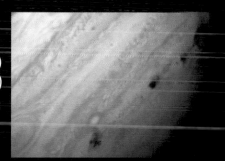

Comet killer

In 1994, Jupiter pulled the comet Shoemaker-Levy 9 to its doom. This caused the largest explosion ever seen in the solar system.

1,321:
the number of Earths Jupiter could swallow

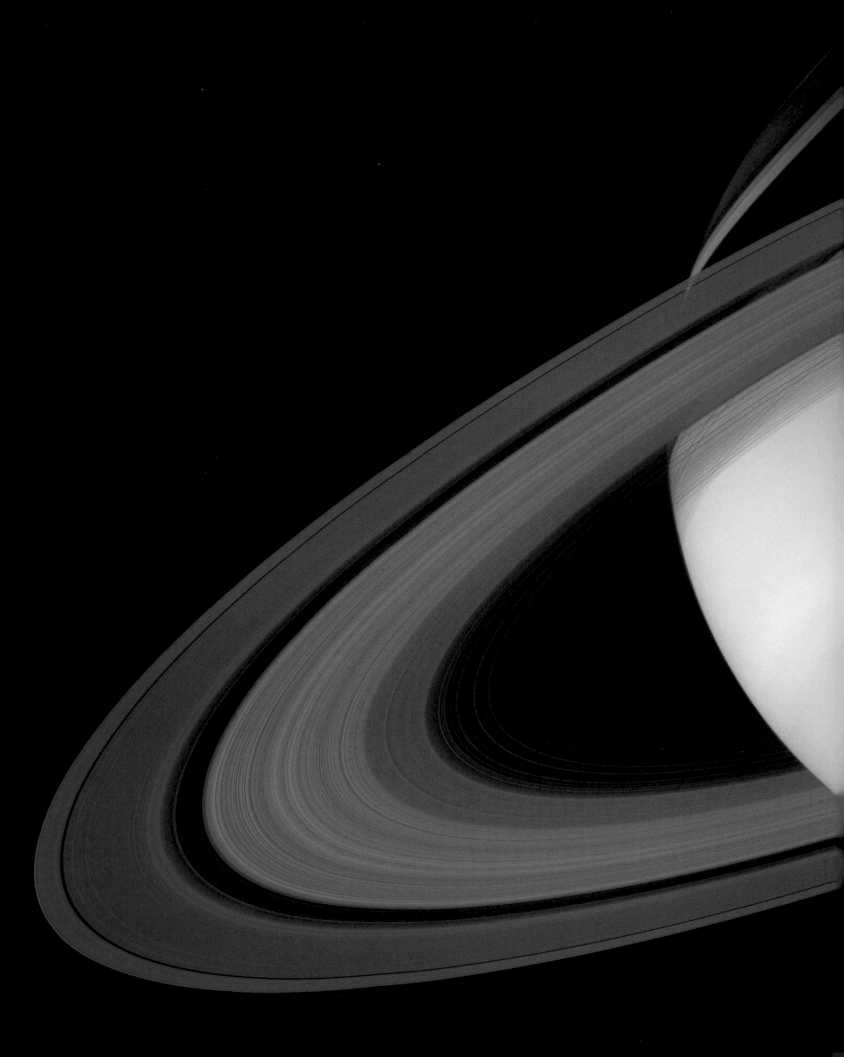

Saturn's rings

Saturn, the most distant planet visible to the naked eye, is best known for its spectacular rings. All the giant planets have ring systems made up of fragments of rock and ice, but Saturn's rings are the most impressive, with a diameter of 280,000 kilometres (174,000 miles). The image, left, was taken by NASA's *Cassini* space probe in orbit around Saturn. It shows both the rings and the deep shadows they cast on Saturn's surface.

OCTOBER 1996

OCTOBER 1997

OCTOBER 1998

NOVEMBER 1999

NOVEMBER 2000

Changing view

Saturn's axis is tilted at 26 degrees, so we see it from different angles as it orbits the Sun. This affects how the rings appear to us.

Outer planets [Icy]

The solar system's outermost planets, Uranus and Neptune, are sometimes called the ice giants, because below their surfaces are layers of water and ice. Beyond Neptune lies the Kuiper Belt, a cloud of small ice dwarfs that includes Pluto.

Uranus

The first planet to be discovered with a telescope, Uranus was spotted in 1781 by astronomer William Herschel, using a telescope he built himself in his back garden in Bath, England. In fact, Uranus is just about bright enough to see with the naked eye, if you know where to look.

Herschel's telescopes
German-born astronomer William Herschel built over 400 telescopes.

Placid world
The *Voyager 2* space probe flew past Uranus for the first time in 1986. It revealed an apparently featureless planet about half the size of Saturn, with a pale blue atmosphere.

Uranus

Diameter	51,118 km (31,763 miles) – 4.01 x Earth
Mass (compared to Earth)	14.5 x Earth
Gravity (compared to Earth)	0.89 x Earth
Rotation period (day)	17 hours, 14 minutes
Number of moons	27

WHAT YOU CAN SEE

Viewing notes
It is possible to spot Uranus using binoculars, but you will see more if you look through a telescope. It looks like a blue-green disk.

🔭 Telescope

The length of winter on Uranus: 42 years

Rings
Uranus is surrounded by a system of 13 narrow rings.

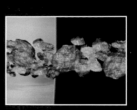

Dark rings
Uranus has dark rings that are composed of large chunks of frozen methane.

Colourful planet
Methane in Uranus' atmosphere absorbs red light, so the planet appears to be a blue-green colour.

Winter at north pole

Summer at south pole

Spring/ Autumn

Sun

Summer at north pole

Spring/ Autumn

Winter at south pole

Strange seasons
Uranus' extreme tilt causes a particular pole to point to the Sun for many years, causing strange seasons. Each pole has 42 years of daylight followed by 42 years of night.

Bright clouds
The highest clouds on Uranus appear white. The lowest clouds appear dark blue.

Changing weather
Observations from Earth have shown that Uranus is far stormier now than it was in the 1980s, and that it has bright clouds. Its weather changes with its long seasons.

Neptune

Discovered in 1846, Neptune is slightly smaller than Uranus and a slightly deeper blue. It is a much more active world, with the highest winds in the solar system and dark storms raging in its atmosphere.

Neptune

Neptune	
Diameter	49,495 km (30,755 miles) – 3.89 x Earth
Mass (compared to Earth)	17.1 x Earth
Gravity (compared to Earth)	1.14 x Earth
Rotation period (day)	16 hours, 7 minutes
Number of moons	13

WHAT YOU CAN SEE

Viewing notes
If you can find Uranus, you can usually find Neptune, too. It is best spotted with a small telescope, using a locator chart. It appears faint and bluish.

Telescope

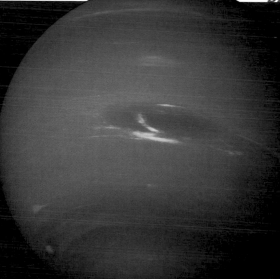

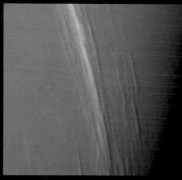

Clouds over Neptune
Streams of bright clouds stretch around Neptune at high altitude, casting their shadows onto the deeper blue atmosphere below.

Great Dark Spot
Voyager 2 discovered a huge storm on Neptune in 1989, but it seems these big storms last only a few years.

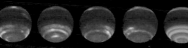

CHANGING WEATHER ON NEPTUNE

2,200 kph **(1,367 mph): the speed of storm winds on Neptune**

Pluto

Tiny Pluto was discovered in 1930 after a deliberate search and was classified as a planet until 2006. Although we now know that it is just one of many ice dwarfs, its icy surface and thin atmosphere are still fascinating. It isn't possible to see Pluto through even a large backyard telescope, because it blends in among countless faint stars.

Pluto and its moons
Charon, Pluto's largest moon, is half the size of its parent planet, and the two keep the same faces permanently turned towards each other. Pluto has at least three other small moons.

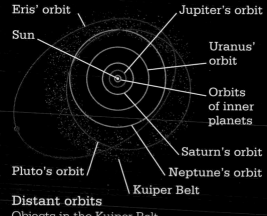

Charon

Hydra

Pluto

Pluto

Pluto	
Diameter	2,322 km (1,442 miles) – 0.18 x Earth
Mass (compared to Earth)	0.002 x Earth
Gravity (compared to Earth)	0.07 x Earth
Rotation period (day)	6 days, 9 hours
Number of moons	4

The Kuiper Belt

Around and beyond the orbit of Neptune lie countless smaller icy worlds, in a doughnut-shaped ring called the Kuiper Belt. These ice dwarfs range from small rocks to worlds larger than Pluto – such as Eris, discovered in 2005.

Eris' orbit

Jupiter's orbit

Sun

Uranus' orbit

Orbits of inner planets

Saturn's orbit

Pluto's orbit

Neptune's orbit

Kuiper Belt

Distant orbits
Objects in the Kuiper Belt take centuries to orbit the Sun. Eris takes 557 years.

Earth isn't the only planet that has a moon. Five other planets have families of moons, ranging from tiny captured asteroids to complex worlds that can be as large as planets themselves.

Phobos

Europa

Io

Mars

Mars has 2 moons, Phobos and Deimos. They look like asteroids, but they may have formed in the same way as Earth's Moon, after a large impact.

Doomed moon
The larger Martian moon, Phobos, will one day crash into Mars.

Jupiter

Jupiter has a huge family of 63 satellites, including 4 giant moons that can be seen with binoculars, and many other smaller ones.

Volcano world
Heated by Jupiter's gravity, Io is the most volcanic world in the solar system.

Ice ball
Europa's smooth, icy surface conceals a deep ocean of water heated by undersea volcanoes.

Mimas

Enceladus

Saturn

Saturn's family of 62 moons ranges from giant Titan (which can be seen with a small telescope) and icy Enceladus to tiny worlds that orbit within the planet's rings (see page 83).

Uranus

Uranus has 27 moons: 13 small ones orbit in and around its rings, 5 in the middle are quite large and icy, and 9 more that orbit much farther out are probably captured comets.

Death star
Mimas' giant crater Herschel was formed by an impact almost big enough to shatter the moon.

Snowy landscape
Heated by tides from Saturn, water from icy Enceladus erupts, freezes instantly, and falls back to the surface as snow.

Triton

Neptune

Neptune has 13 known moons. The icy moon Triton orbits in the wrong direction. It is probably a captured ice dwarf (see page 85) from the Kuiper Belt.

Deep freeze
Neptune's largest moon, Triton, is colder than any other object in the solar system. It has a surface temperature of −235°C (−391°F).

Ganymede

Callisto

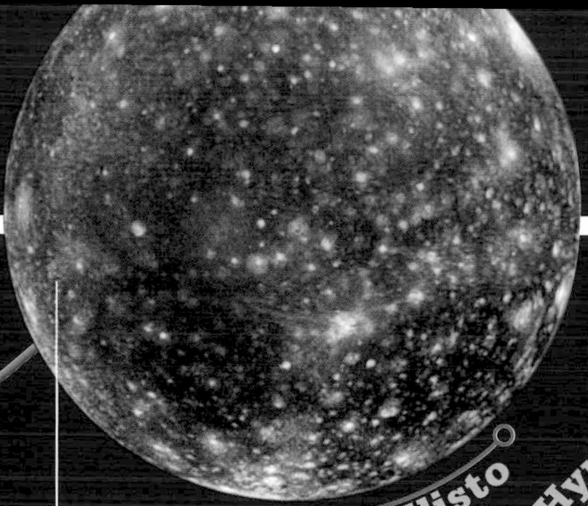

Hyperion

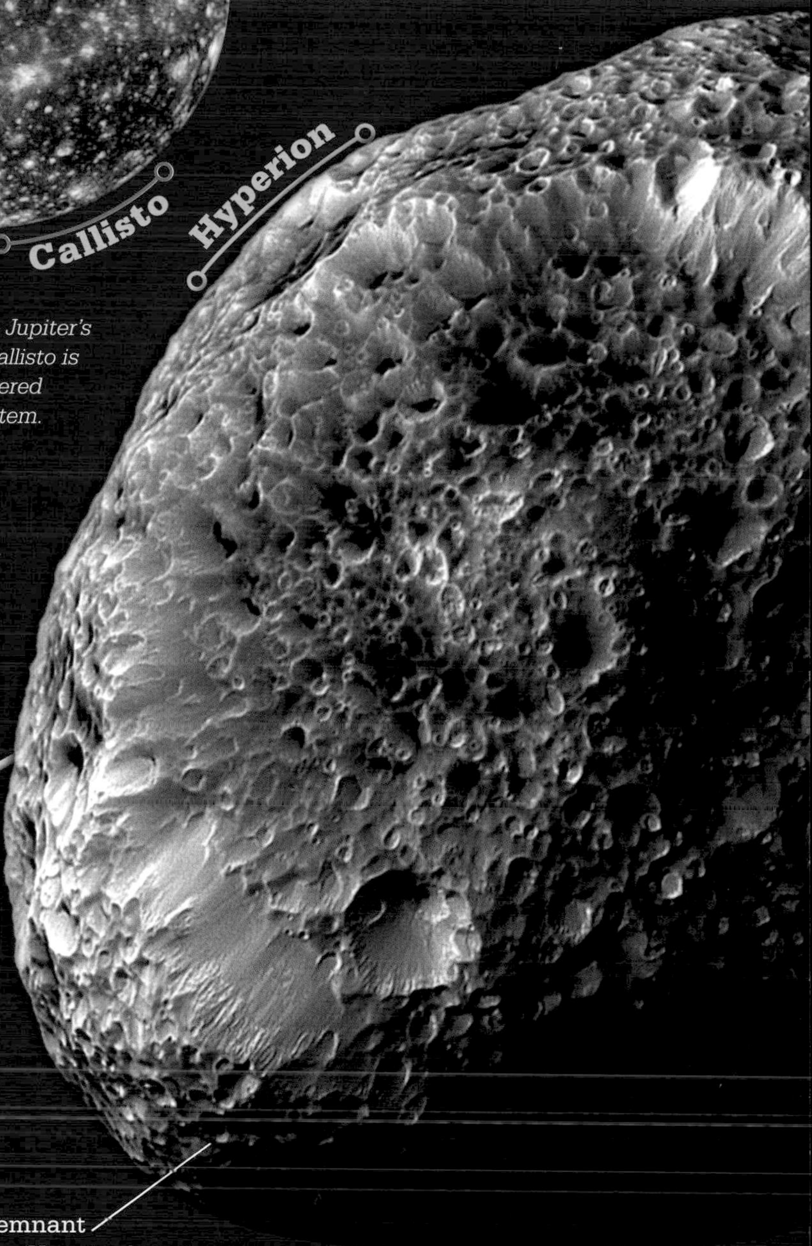

Titan

Miranda

Crater world
Inactive compared to Jupiter's other giant moons, Callisto is the most heavily cratered world in the solar system.

Jumbled surface
Ganymede has a complex surface that has evolved over time.

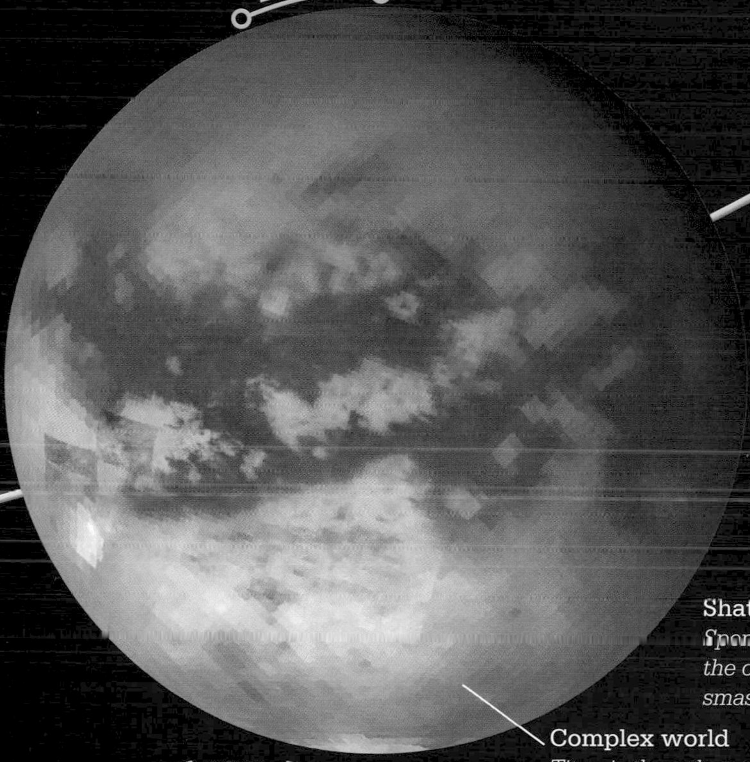

Shattered remnant
Spongy-looking Hyperion began as the core of a larger moon that was smashed apart by a giant impact.

Complex world
Titan is the only moon with an atmosphere, beneath which lies an Earth-like surface with lakes of liquid chemicals.

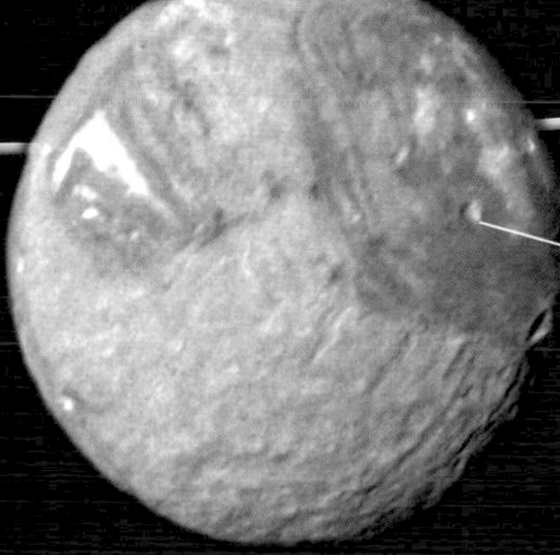

Frankenstein moon
Miranda's mixed-up landscape is so weird that astronomers think it was almost torn apart by tidal forces before reassembling itself.

Jupiter's moon
Ganymede is the
biggest of all: its diameter is
5,260 km (3,268 miles)

In addition to the planets and their moons, smaller objects in our solar system also orbit the Sun. These range from small, rocky asteroids in the warm inner region of the solar system, to icy comets that spend most of their time on the cold edges, although they occasionally come closer to the Sun and warm up.

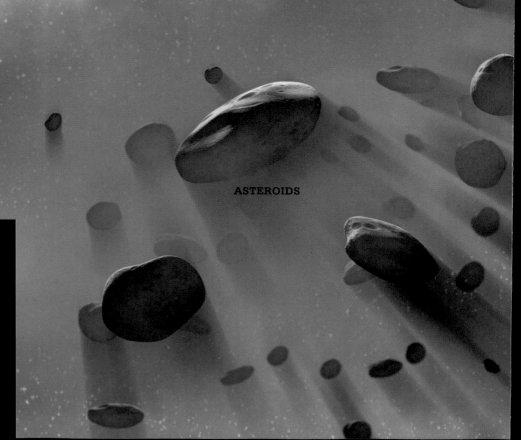

COMET

SUN

ASTEROIDS

Asteroid belt

Most asteroids are found in the asteroid belt, which is a region between the orbits of Mars and Jupiter. The largest known asteroid is Ceres, which has a diameter of 950 km (590 miles). Asteroids are debris left over from the solar system's formation. Jupiter's powerful gravity prevented them from consolidating into a planet.

MARS

Comets

Most comets orbit beyond Neptune, in the Kuiper Belt (see page 85) or even farther out in a region called the Oort Cloud. Occasionally – when they are disturbed – they fall towards the Sun, which melts the ice inside them and causes them to develop extended halos and tails.

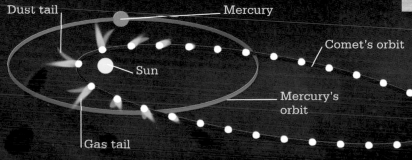

Dust tail

Mercury

Sun

Comet's orbit

Mercury's orbit

Gas tail

Halley's Comet
Halley's Comet passes the Sun every 76 years. Its appearance in 1066 was sewn into the Bayeux Tapestry, a French historical record.

Comet's tail
Solar wind (see page 36) always blows a comet's tail away from the Sun. Comets often have two tails, one made of gas and one of dust.

Galaxies
Univ

- * How old is the Universe?

- * What's on course to collide with the Milky Way?

- * Can anything escape a black hole?

and the

erse

Our galaxy [The Milky Way]

All the stars we can see in the sky are just a tiny fraction of those in our galaxy, the Milky Way. This enormous spiral galaxy is home to our Sun and its solar system, including Earth.

You are here

By measuring the distance and distribution of stars around the Milky Way, astronomers know that our Sun is an insignificant star. It lies near a spiral arm 26,000 light-years (see page 49) from the centre of the Milky Way, roughly halfway across a broad disk that is 100,000 light-years across.

Our solar system
The Sun and its planets are located about halfway between the centre and an edge of the galaxy.

Milky Way galaxy
This illustration shows the Milky Way, looking towards the packed stars of the central bulge.

400,000,000,000

Band across the sky
This panoramic photograph shows the entire Milky Way wrapping around the sky, as seen from Earth. The brightest star clouds and nebulae lie towards the middle of our galaxy.

Shapes in space

Different stars dominate various parts of the Milky Way. Old red and yellow stars are packed in the central bulge, while newer ones circle in a flattened disk. Hot blue and white stars are concentrated in the spiral arms.

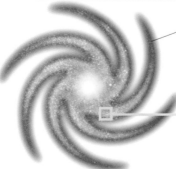

Spiral arms
The arms are not fixed structures – they are concentrations of bright stars.

OVERHEAD VIEW

Oval shape
From the side, the Milky Way looks like a pair of back-to-back fried eggs.

SIDE VIEW

Central bulge
Yellow and red stars orbit in an oval clump.

The Carina Nebula
Newborn stars emerge along the spiral arms. The brightest stars live and die before they can ever move out of the arms.

Our view

When we look in some directions from Earth, we see across the Milky Way, so we see lots of stars behind one another, forming dense star clouds. In other directions, we are looking beyond the Milky Way and so see fewer stars.

Looking out from Earth
As we look in different directions, we see very different views of the Milky Way.

Viewing up
Look past the stars of the Milky Way and you will see the space betweeen our galaxy and others.

Earth

Viewing across
Countless stars form a bright, cloudlike band across the sky.

WHAT YOU CAN SEE

👁 Eye view | 🔭 Telescope

Viewing notes
From a dark location, you can see the pale band of the Milky Way, striped by dark rifts of light-absorbing dust clouds that lie in front of it. If you look through binoculars or a telescope, you will be able to see that the band is made up of countless separate stars.

the number of stars in the Milky Way

Dark heart

The core of the Milky Way, 26,000 light-years from Earth, is held together by an enormous black hole (see pages 60–61), which has the mass of several million Suns. Stars in the central bulge orbit the black hole and stay out of its reach, but it still gives off radio waves as gas drifts into its grasp and heats up.

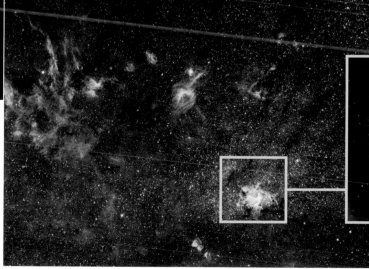

An infrared view of the galaxy
Dense star clouds prevent us from seeing all the way inside our galaxy in visible light, but infrared views can reveal hidden features, such as these dust clouds.

Centre of the Milky Way
This X-ray view shows the very heart of our galaxy. We can see the hot gas clouds surrounding the central black hole, known as Sagittarius A* (pronounced "A-star").

The Milky Way
On a dark, moonless night on Réunion Island in the Indian Ocean, Earth's galaxy, the Milky Way, stretches in a spectacular band across the sky. Brilliant blues and whites indicate the brightest young star clusters. The pinkish patches are nebulae (see page 40), where new stars are born.

Cloud galaxies [Neighbours]

The Milky Way is so huge that its gravity pulls smaller galaxies into orbit around it. The largest of these are irregular galaxies called the Large and Small Magellanic Clouds.

Magellan's galaxies

The clouds were known to people in the Southern Hemisphere for thousands of years. The first European to record them was Portuguese navigator Ferdinand Magellan, on an around-the-world voyage in 1519–22.

180°
Milky Way
270°
90°
0°

Large Magellanic Cloud

Small Magellanic Cloud

Far away
The Large Cloud lies 180,000 light-years, and the Small Cloud 210,000 light-years, from the centre of the Milky Way.

Scale: 100,000 light-years

Large Magellanic Cloud (LMC)

The Large Cloud is both closer to Earth and measurably larger than the other cloud, at about 14,000 light-years across. It is rich in gas, dust, star-forming regions, and newborn heavyweight stars. Many of its stars are lined up along a central bar, and it may have just a single spiral arm.

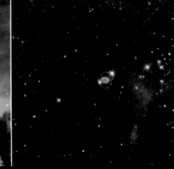

NGC 2074 star cluster
Formation of this cluster may have been triggered by the shockwave from a supernova (see page 58).

Supernova 1987A
A glowing ring marks the remains of a star that exploded in 1987.

Fragmented clouds
Both Magellanic Clouds lie in the far southern skies, as seen from Earth. To observers south of the Equator, they look like separate parts of the Milky Way.

WHAT YOU CAN SEE

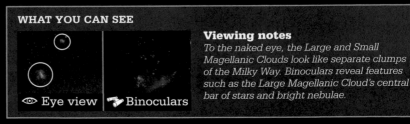

Eye view   Binoculars

Viewing notes
To the naked eye, the Large and Small Magellanic Clouds look like separate clumps of the Milky Way. Binoculars reveal features such as the Large Magellanic Cloud's central bar of stars and bright nebulae.

Tarantula Nebula
This large star-forming region is just above the LMC's central bar of stars.

R136 star cluster
This cluster at the heart of the Tarantula Nebula contains the most massive stars known.

Small Magellanic Cloud (SMC)

The SMC is only about 7,000 light-years across. It is not as structured as the LMC, but it is full of star-forming material and brilliant young stars. It may have started life as a small spiral galaxy before being disrupted by the Milky Way's gravity.

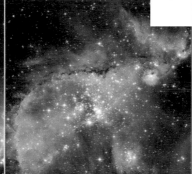

NGC 602
This young star cluster has hollowed out a cavern in the surrounding gas clouds.

NGC 346
Radiation from this star cluster sculpts the glowing clouds of gas around it.

Cannibal galaxy

The Milky Way's gravity doesn't just trap smaller galaxies in orbit, it tears them to shreds and gobbles them up. Astronomers think that the huge globular cluster Omega Centauri is the stripped-down core of a previous galaxy.

OMEGA CENTAURI

The **supernova** 1987A in the Large Magellanic Cloud was the brightest exploding star seen for more than **400 years**

An enormous spiral 2.5 million light-years from Earth, the Andromeda galaxy is even bigger than the Milky Way. It is the farthest night-sky object visible with the naked eye.

Giant spiral
From our location in the Milky Way, we see Andromeda (catalogued as M31) at a shallow angle, with dark dust lanes outlining its spiral structure. Like our own galaxy, Andromeda is orbited by several satellites, including bright balls of stars called M32 and NGC 205.

First sightings
The Andromeda galaxy was recorded by medieval Arab astronomers. Its spiral structure, however, wasn't known until the 19th century. Astronomers couldn't agree on its distance or size.

Arab depiction
Astronomer Abd al-Rahman al-Sufi's *Book of Fixed Stars* has the earliest-known descriptions and illustrations of Andromeda.

How far is Andromeda?
Astronomer Edwin Hubble proved that Andromeda lies far beyond our galaxy by looking for unstable stars called Cepheids. The way they vary reveals their true brightnesses; Hubble used these findings to figure out the real distances of these stars.

Pulsating stars
A Cepheid's brightness and size change in a cycle linked to its true luminosity.

The Local Group
The Milky Way and Andromeda are the two biggest galaxies in the Local Group. This group is a cluster of around 50 galaxies spread across about 10 million light-years of space.

Milky Way
180°
270°   90°
0°
Andromeda galaxy (M31)
Scale: 1 million light-years
LOCATION OF ANDROMEDA

WHAT YOU CAN SEE

<◉> Eye view

Viewing notes
Andromeda is easy to spot in dark skies, even without binoculars or a telescope. You can see it as a fuzzy blob in the sky to the northeast of the square of Pegasus (see page 25).

Andromeda and the Milky Way will collide with each other in about

5 billion years

Galaxies galore [Swirls of stars]

The Universe is filled with hundreds of billions of galaxies, each containing stars, gas, and dust. Galaxies come in many shapes and sizes, from complex spirals to huge oval balls of stars called ellipticals to tiny, irregular dwarf galaxies.

Colliding galaxies

Relative to their enormous sizes, galaxies are surprisingly close together in space, separated by distances equal to just a few times their own diameter. As a result, collisions are common. Astronomers think that collisions cause the different galaxy types in Hubble's classification system (see opposite page).

Galaxy clusters

Galaxies are so massive and have such powerful gravity that they are attracted to one another. They tend to form loose groups, such as our own Local Group (see page 98), and bigger clusters of hundreds of galaxies. Groups of dense clusters, known as superclusters, are the largest things in the Universe.

Abell 2218 galaxy cluster
This galaxy cluster, 2 billion light-years away, contains several thousand galaxies.

800,000,000,000:
the number of galaxies in the Universe

Edwin Hubble

In 1925, US astronomer Edwin Hubble proved that galaxies are star systems far beyond the Milky Way. He later invented a system for classifying different types of galaxy.

Edwin Hubble
Hubble not only discovered the true scale of the Universe, he also proved that it is expanding.

Mice galaxies
This stunning pair of spirals is 300 million light-years from Earth. As the two galaxies collided, their spiral arms unwound to create extended tails.

Key: Galaxies

Barred spiral galaxy	
Spiral galaxy	
Giant elliptical galaxy	
Lenticular galaxy	
Irregular galaxy	
Radio galaxy	
Blazar galaxy	
Quasar galaxy	
Seyfert galaxy	

Classifying galaxies

Hubble's system labels galaxies as barred spirals (such as our Milky Way), normal spirals, ball-like ellipticals, armless spirals called lenticulars, or shapeless clouds of gas and stars called irregulars.

BARRED SPIRAL GALAXY (NGC 1300)

SPIRAL GALAXY (M81)

GIANT ELLIPTICAL GALAXY (M87)

LENTICULAR GALAXY (NGC 2787)

IRREGULAR GALAXY (NGC 1427A)

Active galaxies

As a galaxy's central black hole (see pages 60–61) consumes material that drifts close to it, the galaxy can emit bright light and other kinds of radiation. Astronomers have identified four major types of active galaxy, as shown below.

RADIO GALAXY

BLAZAR GALAXY

QUASAR GALAXY

SEYFERT GALAXY

Glorious galaxies

This image, taken by the Hubble Space Telescope, shows faraway galaxies stretching across the Universe. The most distant objects are billions of light-years away, allowing us to look back in time (see pages 104–105). We can see back to when large galaxies, like those we know today, were being formed by galactic collisions.

By looking out across billions of light-years of space, we can begin to understand the structure of our Universe and its possible origins.

Cosmic time machine

Due to the speed of light (see page 49), the farther we look into space, the further back we can see in time. When we look across billions of light-years, we can see a young Universe that has violent quasars (see page 101), bright irregular galaxies, and galactic collisions.

Deepest view
The farthest galaxies we can see are about 13 billion light-years away. We see them in the process of formation, when the Universe was much younger.

Our Universe is

The big bang

Scientists have calculated that our Universe began 13.7 billion years ago in a huge explosion – the big bang. This created all the energy and matter in the Universe, as well as all time and space.

First stars
Eventually, clouds of matter joined to form the first enormous stars.

First galaxies
Galaxies began to form around the black holes left by the first stars.

Ultra-deep field
The most distant Hubble photos see back to this period, 13.2 billion years ago.

Hubble deep field
The first deep images from the Hubble Space Telescope looked back 12 billion years.

the big bang

The cooling afterglow of the big bang can be seen in the soft glow of radio waves all over the sky.

For 200 million years, there were no stars, and the Universe went through a dark age.

BIG BANG

DARK AGE OF THE UNIVERSE

500–700 MILLION YEARS LATER

1.7 BILLION YEARS LATE

Cosmic expansion

Everything in the Universe is rushing away from everything else. The farther away a galaxy is, the faster it's moving away. Although it's hard to imagine, the Universe is expanding like an inflating balloon!

Tracking back

Cosmic expansion means that at some time in the distant past, everything in the Universe was tightly packed together.

Tight squeeze
In the distant past, galaxies were much closer together.

Big bang

Galaxies expand
In the present-day Universe, galaxies are spaced out.

13.7 billion
years old

Active galaxies
We are much more likely to see violent, active galaxies the farther away we look.

Hubble Telescope
Launched in 1990, this orbiting space telescope provides deep views of the early Universe.

Across the Universe
With powerful technology, we can see to the edge of time and space to detect light and radio waves from just after the big bang itself.

Earth

modern age

13.7 BILLION YEARS LATER

More here

Really, Really Big Questions About Space and Time by Mark Brake

Hubble deep field
active galaxies
cosmic expansion
ultra-deep field
cosmic microwave background

The Universe: Seasons 1, 2 and 3 (The History Channel)

Visit the Jodrell Bank Centre for Astrophysics in Cheshire, which is the global headquarters of the world's next generation radio telescope, the £1.3 billion Square Kilometre Array (SKA).

quasar: the bright centre of a galaxy, believed to be powered by a massive black hole.

radio wave: a ray with the longest wavelength of all. Radio waves are given out by many objects in space.

Array
A group of telescopes that work together to look at the sky at the same time.

Asterism
A cluster of stars that forms an easily recognized pattern.

Asteroid
A chunk of rock left over from the birth of the solar system that is in orbit around the Sun.

Astronomer
A scientist who studies the stars and other objects in space.

Astronomical unit (AU)
A unit equal to he distance from Earth to the Sun, equivalent to 150 million km (93 million miles).

Atmosphere
The layer of gases that surrounds a planet or star. The Earth's atmosphere is the air.

Atom
A tiny particle of matter, consisting of protons, neutrons, and electrons. Atoms are the smallest particles that can take part in a chemical reaction.

Aurora borealis
Also called the northern lights, this is a series of glowing lights in the sky caused by particles from the Sun entering Earth's atmosphere.

Axis
An imaginary straight line from the top to the bottom of a spinning object such as Earth. The object rotates around the axis.

Binary star
A double star system, in which one star orbits the other.

Black hole
The superdense collapsed core of a burnt-out star. It sucks in every object around it in space. It even pulls back rays of light. This is why we cannot see a black hole with our eyes.

Blazar
An active galaxy shooting a jet of material straight towards Earth.

Celestial pole
The points in the celestial sphere directly above Earth's poles, around which the sphere seems to spin as Earth rotates.

Celestial sphere
An imaginary shell around the sky, on which the movements of stars and planets can be mapped.

Cepheid
A type of star that pulsates as it changes its size and brightness over a given period.

Cluster
A group of stars or galaxies.

Comet
A chunk of frozen gas and dust that travels in an elongated orbit around the Sun. When it warms up near the Sun, dust and vapour streams out behind the comet to produce a spectacular "tail".

Constellation
One of 88 divisions of the sky used by astronomers, or the patterns of stars within these divisions.

Core
The centre of a star or planet, where matter is hottest and most compressed.

Crater
A bowl-shaped depression in a planetary surface, often hollowed out by a meteorite impact.

Dry ice
Carbon dioxide gas in its solid, frozen form.

Dwarf galaxy
A small galaxy, usually either ball shaped or irregular.

Eclipse
An event in which three astronomical bodies line up with each other – for instance when the Moon passes in front of the Sun as seen from Earth, or the Earth passes between the Sun and the Moon.

Ecliptic
The Sun's path around the celestial sphere each year.

Electron
A lightweight particle with negative electric charge, found inside an atom.

Elliptical
Elongated, as in the shape of a comet's orbit or some galaxies.

Event horizon
A barrier around a black hole marking the point where nothing can escape its gravity.

Far side
The side of the Moon that is permanently turned away from Earth.

Focus
The point in a telescope where light rays come together so that an image can be seen clearly.

Galaxy
A huge structure of stars, gas, and dust, usually in the shape of a spiral, an elliptical ball, or an irregular cloud.

Gas giant
An enormous planet that has a small solid core surrounded by huge amounts of gas.

Gibbous
The bulging appearance of the Moon when it is bigger than a half-moon, but not yet full.

Globular cluster
A ball-shaped star cluster containing many thousands of very old, yellowish stars.

Gravity
The force that pulls things towards massive objects such as planets and stars.

Helium
A lightweight gas, helium is the second most common element in the Universe.

Hubble Space Telescope
A telescope in orbit around the Earth that provides many of our best views of space objects.

Hydrogen
The lightest and most common element in the Universe, making up the bulk of all stars and interstellar gas.

The surface of the Moon has about the same area as the continent of Africa

Glossary

Ice dwarf
A small icy world orbiting the Sun beyond Neptune.

Infrared
An invisible type of light that is produced by objects that are too cool to glow in visible light. Special cameras can use infrared rays to pick out things that cannot be seen with an ordinary camera.

Interstellar
Describes something that is situated or occurs between the stars.

Lava tube
A tunnel carved out by molten rock flowing in a river underneath a landscape.

Light-year (ly)
The distance travelled by light in one Earth year. One light-year is equivalent to 9.5 million million km (5.9 million million miles).

Long exposure
A technique used in photography when the camera is left open for a long period of time, allowing it to soak up more light than our eyes can detect.

Luminosity
A measure of the energy that is produced by a star; the brightness of a star in comparison with that of the Sun.

Lunar
Concerning Earth's Moon.

Magnetic field
An invisible field around some planets and other objects that affects certain objects that pass nearby.

Magnitude
A measure of a star's brightness. Apparent magnitude is the brightness of a star as seen from Earth.

In 1054 CE, a supernova explosion produced the Crab Nebula

Main sequence star
A star in the longest phase of its life cycle, when it shines because it has a stable nuclear reaction. The star moves off the main sequence when the hydrogen in its core is exhausted.

Meteor
A piece of space debris that burns up as it hits the atmosphere around a planet. Some are huge, others the size of pebbles. As they burn, they make a bright light in the sky.

Meteorite
A piece of space debris that passes through a planet's atmosphere without burning up. It crashes on the surface.

Moon
A large, solid world in orbit around a planet, also called a satellite. The Earth has one Moon. It is a small world with no atmosphere and no life.

Nearside
The side of the Moon that is always turned towards Earth.

Nebula
A cloud of gas and dust in interstellar space, in which stars are born.

Neutron
A particle that has no electrical charge, slightly bigger than a proton. There are neutrons in the nuclei of all atoms except those of hydrogen.

Neutron star
A superdense object formed from the collapsed core of a burnt-out star, it is composed of neutrons, very small, and spins very fast. Neutron stars are often pulsars.

Nuclear fusion
The centre of an atom is called the nucleus. The nuclei of atoms can join together in a process called fusion, which creates the nuclei of heavier atoms and releases a great amount of energy. Fusion makes the Sun burn.

Open cluster
A small star cluster containing a few dozen stars that have formed in the recent past from the same nebula.

Orbit
The path taken by one object around another under the influence of gravity. The Earth moves in orbit round the Sun.

Phase
The amount of a planet or moon that is lit by the Sun as seen from another area of space.

Photosphere
The brilliant outer surface of the Sun that we can see. It is made of hot gases and gives off almost all the light we get from the Sun.

Planet
A body in space that moves in orbit around a star such as the Sun. Planets have no light of their own. They reflect the light of the star around which they are orbiting.

Planetary nebula
The gas shell thrown off when a red star dies.

Polaris
The pole star, or north star – a star that happens to lie very close to the North Celestial Pole.

Probe
An unmanned robot spacecraft that is sent to investigate the planets and other space objects up close.

Proton
A positively charged particle that is found in the nucleus of an atom.

Pulsar
A neutron star with a powerful magnetic field that sends spinning, lighthouse-like beams into space.

Quasar
An active galaxy with a brilliant central region created by a giant black hole (see opposite) that is swallowing stars and heating up gas.

Radiation
Also called electromagnetic radiation, this is a moving electrical and magnetic disturbance that we experience as light and heat.

One year on Mercury is equal to 88 days on Earth

Radio wave
An electromagnetic wave within the range of radio frequencies

Red giant
A giant star towards the end of its life. It has a relatively low temperature and emits a red light.

Reflecting telescope
A telescope that makes a bright, magnified image by collecting light with mirrors.

Refracting telescope
A telescope that makes a bright, magnified image by collecting light with lenses.

Satellite
A small body that orbits a much larger one in space under the influence of the larger one's gravity. Satellites can be either natural (moons) or artificial.

Shooting star
A bright streak of light in the sky caused by a meteor hitting air molecules and burning up.

Solar flare
A sudden eruption of hydrogen gas in the Sun's atmosphere caused by changes in the Sun's magnetic field.

Solar system
Everything that is held in orbit around a star such as the Sun by its gravity. Our solar system includes planets, moons, comets, asteroids, ice dwarfs, and other objects.

Solar wind
A stream of particles that blows out across the solar system from the surface of the Sun.

Star
A huge, glowing ball of gas that gives off its own heat and light. The Sun is Earth's star.

Sunspot
A relatively cool patch on the surface of the Sun that appears dark by comparison with its bright surroundings. Sunspots are caused by the Sun's magnetic field.

Supergiant
One of the largest stars known, with a diameter far bigger than Earth's orbit around the Sun.

Supernova
A huge explosion that sometimes outshines all the other stars in a galaxy. Supernovae mark the death of the heaviest stars.

Ultraviolet
An invisible type of light that is produced by objects too hot to glow in visible light.

White dwarf
A hot, dense object the size of the Earth, formed by the core of a burnt-out star such as the Sun.

X-ray
A high-frequency wave of electromagnetic energy. X-rays are given out by some of the most violent processes in the Universe.

Zodiac
The 12 ancient constellations that the Sun passes through each year as it moves along the ecliptic.

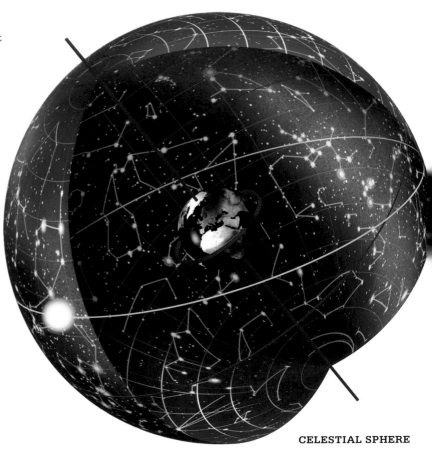

CELESTIAL SPHERE

A

Abell 2218 galaxy cluster 100
Acidalia Planitia, Mars 79
active galaxy 101, 105
Aitken crater, Moon 72
al-Sufi, Abd al-Rahman 98
Albireo (star) 50
Aldebaran (star) 58
Aldrin, Edwin "Buzz" 71
Almagest, the 29
Ancient Egyptian astronomers 23
Andromeda galaxy (M31) 17, 49, 98–99
Antares (star) 52, 53
Apollo space programme 71, 73, 75
Arabic astronomers 23, 98
Archer, the *see* Sagittarius
Argentina, view from 21
Argo (constellations) 27, 45
Armstrong, Neil 71
asteroid 17, 32, 81, 86, 88–89
asteroid belt 88
astronaut 62, 71, 73, 74–75
astronomer 18, 23, 24, 26, 29, 32, 40, 42, 45, 47, 50, 52, 56, 58, 79, 81, 84, 98, 101
astronomical unit (AU) 66
astronomy club 19, 65
Atlas 20
Auriga (constellation) 58
Aurora borealis see also Northern Lights 8–9, 36
autumn, seasonal changes 25, 27
averted vision 16

B

Bayeux Tapestry 89
Betelgeuse (star) 39, 40
big bang 104–105
Big Dipper *see also* Plough 22, 23
binary star 50
binoculars 16–17, 18
black hole 60–61
    active galaxy 101
    Cygnus X-1 50, 51, 61
    Milky Way 93
blazar galaxy 101
blue giant 39
blue planet 84–85
blue star 38, 92, 95
brightness 17, 39, 47, 98
Bull, the see Taurus
Butterfly nebula 54–55

C

Callisto (moon of Jupiter) 81, 87
camera, use of 17
Canis Major (constellation) 25, 27, 29, 40
Canis Minor (constellation) 25, 29, 40
Canopus (star) 27, 45
Canyon Diablo, Arizona, USA 32
Carina (constellation) 27, 29, 44–45
Carina nebula 45, 92
Cassini space probe 80, 83
Cat's Paw nebula (NGC 6334) 53
celestial equator 20, 24, 25, 26, 28
celestial globe 23
celestial poles 20, 21, 26
celestial sphere 20–21
Centaurus (constellation) 22, 27
Centaurus A galaxy 19
Cepheids 98
Ceres asteroid 17, 88
Challenger space shuttle 33
Chandrayaan space programme 71
Charon (moon of Pluto) 85
Chinese astronomers 24
Chryse Planitia, Mars 79
cloud galaxy 96–97
colour, stars 25, 38–39
comet
    Hale-Bopp 30–31
    Jupiter 81
    meteor link 32
    orbiting Sun 88–89
    tail 89
constellation 22–23
    equatorial skies 28–29
    Northern hemisphere 24–25
    Southern hemisphere 26–27
    zodiac 28–29
co-ordinate grid 20
Copernicus crater, Moon 70, 72
Crab nebula (M1) 58
crater
    Callisto 87
    Mercury 76
    meteor 32, 33
    Mimas 86
    on Moon 70, 72
Crescent nebula (NGC 6888) 50
Crux Australis see Southern Cross
Crystal Ball nebula 58
Cygnus (constellation), the Swan 25, 28, 50–51

D

Deneb (star) 50, 51
diamond 60
dinosaurs 33, 49
dome telescope 19

E

Eagle nebula (M16) 49
Earth
    see also Moon
    atmosphere 9, 14, 19, 32
    impacts 32, 33, 72
    movement 14
    oceans 64
    orbit 18, 28, 66
    rising over Moon 72
    rocky planet 64
    rotation effect 14, 20, 21
    shadow 14
    size 67
    speed of light 49
    view from 20–21
eclipse 69
ecliptic path 20, 24, 26, 28
Egyptian astronomers 23
electric light 14, 23
elliptical galaxy 101
Enceladus (moon of Saturn) 86
energy, of the Sun 37
Eos Chasma, Mars 79
Epsilon Lyrae (multiple star system) 56, 57
equator
    celestial 20, 24, 25, 26, 28
    star map 28–29
Eridanus (constellation) 61
Eris (dwarf planet) 85
Eta Carinae (star system) 45
Europa (moon of Jupiter) 81, 86

G

galaxy
    active 101, 105
    Andromeda 17, 49, 98–99
    blazar 101
    classification 101
    cloud 96–7
    clustering 10–11, 100
    colliding 99, 100, 103, 104
    elliptical 101
    formation 104
    irregular 101, 104
    lenticular 101
    Local Group 98, 100
    Mice 101
    Milky Way 92–93
    most distant 104
    quasar 101
    radio 101
    Seyfert 101
    spiral 47, 92, 98, 101
    in Universe 100–103
    using telescope to view 17
Galileo Galilei 18, 81
Ganymede (moon of Jupiter) 81, 87
gas cloud see nebula
gas giant 64, 65, 80
globular cluster 42, 52, 96–97
gravitational pull
    asteroid belt 88
    galaxies 10
    Sun 64, 66
Great Bear (constellation), Ursa Major 22, 23, 25, 28, 29
Greek astronomers 23, 40, 42, 45, 47, 50, 52, 56
    Ptolemy's *Almagest* 29
Grimaldi crater, Moon 70

H

Hale-Bopp comet 30–31
Halley's Comet 89
HD 97950 nebula 45
helium 37
hemispheres 20, 21
Heracles see Hercules
Hercules 47
Herschel crater, Mimas 86
Herschel, William 58, 84
Horsehead nebula 40
Hubble, Edwin 98, 101
Hubble Space Telescope 17, 19, 38, 103, 104, 105
Hunter, the see Orion
Hyades star cluster 58
Hydra (moon of Pluto) 85
Hydra (constellation), Water Snake 23
hydrogen 37, 39, 47, 53, 80
Hyperion 87

I

ice giant 84
icy planet 84–85, 86
identification of objects in space 15, 76, 78, 81, 83
India, space programme 71
infrared ray 19, 93
invisible light 19
Io (moon of Jupiter) 81, 86
Iraq, star chart 29
irregular galaxy 101, 104
Irwin, James 74–75

J

Jodrell Bank 19, 105
Jupiter 65, 67, 80–81
    asteroid belt 88
    identifying 14, 17

Index

moons 17, 81, 86–87
red spots 80

K

Kasei Valles, Mars 79
Keel, the see Carina
constellation
Kepler crater, Moon 70
Kuiper Belt 85, 89

L

Lacaille, Nicolas Louis
de 26
Lagoon nebula (M8)
42, 43
Large Magellanic
Cloud (LMC) 96
lens-based telescopes
18
lenticular galaxies
101
Leo (constellation), the
Lion 23, 24, 27, 29,
46–47
Libra constellation 53
light
from the Sun 36
invisible 19
pollution 14, 23
speed of 49, 104
visible 19
light year (ly) 49
Local Group 98, 100
location, differing sky
views 21
Luna space missions
71
Lunae Planum, Mars
79
Lunar Apennine
mountains, Moon 71,
73
Hadley Mountain,
Moon 73, 75
lunar rover 71, 72
Lunar Roving Vehicle
71, 74–75
Lunokhod space
missions 71
Lyra (constellation),
25, 28, 56–57

M

M1 (Crab nebula) 58
M4 star cluster 52, 53
M8 nebula 42, 43
M16 nebula 49
M17 nebula 42, 43
M20 nebula 42, 43
M25 star cluster 49
M31 (Andromeda) 17,
49, 98–99
M32 stars 98
M45 (Pleiades) 17, 58
M56 star cluster 56
M57 Ring nebula 17,
56, 57
M65 galaxy 47
M66 galaxy 47
M81 galaxy 101
M87 galaxy 17, 101
M95 galaxy 47
M96 galaxy 47
M101 galaxy 17
M105 galaxy 47
Magellan, Ferdinand,
cloud galaxies 27,
96–97
magnitude bar 17
Mars 64, 66, 67, 78–79
asteroid belt 88
identifying 15
moons 86–87
Mercury 64, 66, 67, 76
Messenger spacecraft
76
Messier object 87 17
meteor 15, 32–33
meteorite 32–33, 72,
73
Mice galaxy 101
Milky Way 92–95
cloud galaxies 96–97
identification of 15,
17
Local Group 98
Southern hemisphere
22, 27
Mimas 86
Miranda, moon of
Uranus 87
Moon buggy see Lunar
rover
Moon, the 68–69

craters 70, 72
eclipses 69
exploration 71, 72,
75
far side 70, 71
formation 72
map 70–71
monthly cycle 68–69
mountains 70, 71,
73
orbit 68–69
rising location 14
rocks 73
seas 70, 71, 72
seeing details of
surface 16–17, 70
moons
of Jupiter 17, 81,
86–87
of Mars 86–87
of Neptune 86–87
of Pluto 85
of Saturn 86–87
of Uranus 86–87
myths 20, 47, 50, 53,
72, 87

N

naked eye, objects
14, 16–17, 76, 83
NASA
Cassini space probe
80, 83
Challenger, damage
to 33
Kids' Club 65
space telescopes 19
Nebra sky disk 58
nebula
Butterfly 54–55
Carina 45, 92
Crab 58
Cygnus 50
Milky Way 95
Orion 40
planetary 39
Ring 17, 56, 57
Sagittarius 42, 43
Scorpius 53
Neptune 65, 67, 85
distance from Sun
48

identification of 17
moons 86–87
speed of light 49
neutron stars 60, 61
Newton, Isaac 18
NGC 205 stars 98
NGC 346 star cluster
97
NGC 406 galaxy 49
NGC 602 star cluster
97
NGC 1300 galaxy
101
NGC 1427A galaxy
101
NGC 2074 star cluster
96
NGC 2787 galaxy 101
NGC 3603 star cluster
45
NGC 3628 galaxy 47
NGC 6334 nebula 53
NGC 6357 nebula 53
NGC 6822 galaxy 42
NGC 6888 nebula 50
NGC 6992 nebula 50,
51
NGC 7000 nebula 50,
51
North America nebula
(NGC 7000) 50, 51
North Pole 24, 25
North Star see Polaris
Northern Cross see
Cygnus
Northern hemisphere
21, 24–25
Northern lights see
also Aurora borealis
8–9, 36
nuclear fusion 37,
39, 47

O

objective lens 18
objects
identification of 15,
76, 78, 81, 83
movement 14,
20–21
Northern hemisphere
24–25

size 48–49, 66–67, 81
Southern hemisphere
26–27
Olympus Mons, Mars
78, 79
Omega Centauri 97
Omega nebula (M17)
42, 43
Oort Cloud 49, 89
open cluster 42
Ophiuchus
(constellation), the
Serpent Bearer 29
orange star 38
Orion (constellation),
the Hunter 24, 25,
27, 29, 40–1, 53
Orpheus 56

P

Pegasus (constellation)
25, 28
Phaeton 50, 53
Phobos, moon of Mars
86
photography 17
photosphere 36
planetarium 65
planetary nebula 39,
56, 60, 61
planets 64–65
distance from Earth
48, 66–67
gas giant 64, 65, 80
icy 84–85
identification of 15,
76, 78, 81, 83,
84–85
orbit 64, 66–67,
76
rings 83
rocky 64
size viewed from
Earth 48, 66–67
Plato crater, Moon 70
Pleiades (M45) 17, 58
Plough see also Big
Dipper 23
Pluto (dwarf planet)
85
Polaris 21, 24, 25
pollution, light 14, 23

primary mirror 18
Proxima Centauri 48,
49
Ptolemy 29
pulsar 61
pulsating star 98
Puppis (star) 27

Q

quasar galaxy 101,
104, 105

R

R136 star cluster 97
radio galaxy 101
radio telescope 19,
105
radio waves 19, 61,
93, 104, 105
red dwarf 39
red giant 38, 39, 53,
56
red star 38
reflecting telescope 18
refractor telescope 18
Regulus 46, 47
Rigel 39, 40
Ring nebula (M57) 17,
56, 57
rings
Saturn 82–83
Uranus 84
rocky planet 64
Russia, space
programme 71, 77

S

Sagittarius A* black
hole 93
Sagittarius
(constellation), the
Archer 26, 27,
28, 38, 42–43, 49
San Francisco, view
from 21
satellite 15
Saturn 17, 65, 67,
82–83, 86–87
Schiaparelli, Giovanni
32, 79

Schmitt, Harrison 73
Shoemaker-Levy 9
   comet 81
Schröter's Valley, Moon
   73
Scorpius
   (constellation), the
   Scorpion 26, 27,
   28, 42, 52–55
Sea of Moscow, Moon
   70
seasons
   reasons for 67
   star map changes
      25, 27
   Uranus 84
secondary mirror 18
Serpent Bearer, the
   see Ophiuchus
Seven Sisters see
   Pleiades
Seyfert galaxies 101
Shaula (star) 52, 53
shooting star 15,
   32–33
Sirius (star) 17, 27, 61
size of objects in space
   48–49, 66–67, 81
Small Magellanic
   Cloud (SMC) 27, 96, 97
Smyth's Sea 72
solar flare 36
solar system
   early beliefs 20, 23,
      24, 29
   Galileo's discoveries
      18
   moons 86–87
   planets 64–67
   position in Milky Way
      92
   size 48–49, 66
solar wind 9, 36, 89
South Pole 26, 27
Southern Cross (Crux
   Australis) 22, 26,
   27, 28
Southern hemisphere
   21, 26–27
Soviet Union, space
   programme 71, 77
space probe 77, 80,
   83, 84, 85

space telescope 17,
   19, 38, 103, 104, 105
space travel
   Jupiter 80
   Mars 78
   Mercury 76
   Moon 71, 72, 73
   Neptune 85
   Saturn 83
   size of Universe 48
   space junk 33
   Uranus 84
   Venus 77
space vehicles
   Lunar Rover 71, 72,
      73, 74–75
   Mars 78
spaghettification 60
spiral galaxy 47, 92,
   98, 101
Spitzer Space Telescope
   19
spring, seasonal
   changes 25, 27
star cluster
   Lyra 56
   Magellanic Clouds
      96, 97
   Milky Way 95
   Scorpius 53
   star life cycle 39, 42
   Taurus 58
star map
   equator 28–29
   Northern hemisphere
      24–25
   Southern hemisphere
      26–27
star
   binary 50
   birth 39, 40, 104
   brightness 17, 39,
      47, 98
   colour 25, 38–39
   constellation 22–23,
      24–25
   death 39, 56, 60
   distance 20, 98
   equatorial skies
      28–29
   identification of 15
   life cycle 39, 42, 47
   main sequence 39, 47

in Milky Way 92
motion 20, 21
neutron 60, 61
Northern hemisphere
   24–25
quadruple 56
size 39
Southern hemisphere
   26–27
stationary 21
weight 39, 47, 60
Stephan's Quintet
   10–11
summer, seasonal
   changes 25, 27
Sun 36–37
   distance from
      Earth 48–49, 66
   eclipse 69
   energy 37
   gravity 64, 66
   looking at 17, 19, 37
   movement 18, 20,
      28
   planets orbiting 64,
      66–67
   size viewed from
      Earth 48–49, 66
   structure 36–37
   surface 36
   weight 64
   zodiac signs 28, 29
sunrise 76
sunset 14, 76
sunspots 36, 37
superclusters 100
supergiant 53
Supernova 1987A
   96, 97
supernova 39, 58,
   61
Swan, the see Cygnus
Swan nebula see
   Omega nebula

T
Tarantula nebula 97
Taurus (constellation),
   the Bull 25, 29, 40
Taurus–Littrow region
   73
Teapot (stars) 42–43

telescope
   dome 19
   eyepiece 18
   first use 18
   focus 18
   Herschel's 84
   Hubble Space 17, 19,
      38, 103, 104, 105
   radio 19, 105
   reflecting 18
   refractor 18
   space 17, 19, 38,
      103, 104, 105
   Spitzer Space 19
Tharsis volcano chain
   78
Theia 72
Titan, moon of Saturn
   87
Trifid nebula (M20)
   42, 43
Triton, moon of
   Neptune 86
Tsiolkovskiy crater,
   Moon 70, 72
Tucana (constellation)
   49
Turkey, view from 21
Tycho crater, Moon 70,
   71, 73

U
Universe
   expansion 101, 105
   galaxies 100, 101,
      102–103
   origins 49, 104–105
   size 48–9, 66, 101
Uranus 17, 65, 67, 84,
   86–87
Ursa Major see
   Great Bear
USA, space programme
   71, 73, 75

V
Valles Marineris 79
Vega 56, 57
Veil nebula (NGC 6992)
   50, 51
Vela 27

Venera space probes 77
Venus 15, 17, 64, 66,
   77
viewfinder 18
visible light 19
volcanic activity
   Earth 64
   Io 86
   Mars 78, 79
   Moon 72, 73
   Venus 77
Voyager 2 space probe
   84, 85

W
War of the Worlds, The
   79
watching the sky
   12–17
   constellations 22–29
   equipment 16–17
   identifying objects
      15, 23, 76, 78, 81, 83
   meteors 32–3
   when to watch
      14–15, 23
water
   on Earth 64
   on Enceladus 86
   on Europa 86
   on Mars 78
   on Mercury 76
   on the Moon 71
white dwarf 56, 60, 61
white star 38, 92, 95
Wolf 359 47

X
X-rays 19, 60, 61, 93

Y
yellow star 38

Z
Zeus 50
zodiac constellations
   28–29

Credits and acknowledgment